Beer

History, Legends, Trends

WHITE STAR PUBLISHERS

Contents

Introduction 4

A Little Bit of History 6

Geography 12

Production 18

The Many Styles of Beer 25

TEXT BY PIETRO FONTANA

PHOTOGRAPHS BY FABIO PETRONI

Introduction

A good beer is a simple pleasure, but its history is a surprisingly complex subject. Humans have been drinking beer for centuries, yet its brewing process continues to evolve at a dizzying pace.

It's impossible to talk about beer's relevance to modern society without also delving into its historical significance. Who knows how many geopolitical deals, treaties, and truces have been hashed out over a beer? Every day, new breweries, bars, and pubs open up around the world, many of them determined to invent original ways of brewing, serving, and marketing beer. Modern reinterpretations of classic beer styles are all the rage right now, but brand-new categories are also constantly being invented, forcing beer judges and international competitions to stay on their toes. The rediscovery of extinct regional brewing traditions is another new front in beer brewing, along with hybrid cocktails and the never-ending search for strange new ingredients. And we can't forget the brewing cultures popping up in countries not previously known for beer, including Brazil, Spain, and Iceland. Up until the end of the 17th century, there was a large network of small and independent local producers of beer. Due to gradual improvements in technology, transportation, and beer preservation, the industry began to shrink, with fewer breweries responsible for beer production. By the 1970s, the United States had only 49 breweries operating 94 plants, and these supplied the entire country. In a sense, brewing has come full circle, as the United States now has roughly 7,450 breweries supplying beer to millions of beer enthusiasts.

International beer producers now find themselves compet-
ing with local single-worker brewing operations, but both con-
tribute to the expansion of beer culture. Experimentation and
cutting-edge ingredients are great, but what about the times
when you're in the mood for something familiar? In addition to
introducing you to new, hard-to-find beers, we also cover many
classic styles, as they've done just as much to shape our tastes.
Before moving further into the beer universe, we want to clarify
that the beers covered in this book weren't selected based on
quality alone. Those kinds of lists can be found everywhere, but
they won't teach you much about beer. Instead, we wanted to
offer a glimpse of the industry as a whole, while exposing you
to as many beer varieties as possible. The various beers featured throughout the book fall into a few loose categories. This
approach may offend beer purists, but it allows us to include
many diverse and exciting beers that might otherwise have
been omitted. One example is the section titled "Other Cereal
Grains," which includes a Weizen Doppelbock, a Grodziskie, and
a Blanche/Wit—all very different beers. Lastly, we wanted to say
a few words about the "Borderline Beers" category. This section
features numerous strange and avant-garde brewing trends that
many may consider more in the realm of cocktails or sodas. So
be it. We want to surprise and amaze you, while also widening
your beer imagination. Brewing is rich in history and tradition,
but the best traditions are the result of years of innovation.

A Little Bit of History

The Beginning

Fermenting cereal grains to produce alcoholic drinks dates back to 8,000 BC, in Mesopotamia, and was probably discovered by accident. Mesopotamian engravings depict a goddess called Ninkasi—the first goddess of beer. The oldest recipe for making beer can be found in a hymn dedicated to Ninkasi. The beverage was mainly prepared by women and consumed out of large jugs with long, straw-like devices. After the Babylonians conquered Sumer, they began producing the beverage as well. Brewing is also mentioned in the Code of Hammurabi, which divides beer into twenty different categories.

In Ancient Egypt, beer and bread were sometimes used as forms of currency. Because of its alcohol content, which helped kill germs, beer was actually more hygienic to drink than water at that time. It was consumed by pharaohs and the lower classes alike. The Romans (and the Greeks before them) also brewed beer, but the wealthier classes of the Roman Empire preferred wine, which was celebrated in many popular songs and poems. Beer was thus mainly enjoyed by people in the provinces.

The distinction between wine, the drink of artists, scholars, and the aristocracy, and beer, drunk by illiterate nomads and the lower classes, remained largely unchanged until the fall of the Roman Empire, when drinking beer became a widespread practice. Nomadic Germanic tribes began adding *gruit* to beer, which is a mixture of herbs and plants. Gruit mixtures included ingredients such as juniper berries, ginger, caraway seeds, aniseed, nutmeg, cinnamon, mint, and occasionally hops.

A plate from Treatise on Medicine *by Aldebrando de Firenze (1356) depicting an early brewing process.*

In the Middle Ages, beer also became increasingly widespread thanks to the large number of monasteries and abbeys producing it. Many monasteries established full breweries, with vats for mashing and fermentation and areas designated specifically for malting. Monks were widely considered expert brewers!

A 19th-century closed fermentation tank designed to keep bacteria from spoiling the beer as it fermented.

The Purity Law

In 1516, the Bavarian city of Ingolstadt stipulated that barley was the only acceptable cereal grain for beer. Further, the purity law required that "nothing other than barley, hops, and water [could] be used" to produce beer. However, the use of other cereal grains for brewing was common in other parts of Germany (for example, the wheat used in Weizen beers). The purity law is still respected today by many German brewers. It initially applied only to the Duchy of Bavaria, but since 1906, it has been the law governing beer brewing throughout all of Germany. At the end of the 20th century, the law was loosened to allow for more innovative brewing practices.

The *Reinheitsgebot*, as the law is called, was mainly established for economic and taxation reasons. Many other countries have borrowed from the law in creating their own brewing standards. Germany has thus become synonymous with quality brewing. For many people around the globe, the only beer for them is a German beer. Foreign demand for German beer remains high today, most likely in part due to Germany's strict adherence to its traditional brewing standards.

The Scientific and Industrial Revolutions

But what about yeast? In the original *Reinheitsgebot* document, there is no mention of yeast. Well, that's because yeast had yet to be discovered. Antonie van Leeuwenhoek (1632–1723) was an early microscopist and microbiologist. He was one of the first to observe and describe yeast in the beer fermentation process.

However, the organic nature of yeast wasn't fully understood until the 19th century. Louis Pasteur (1822–1895), the famous French scientist, explained the importance of various microorganisms in fermentation, and this had a massive impact on the beer industry. Pasteur's observations on the role of various microorganisms during fermentation—described in detail in his book *Études sur la Bière* (1876)—are still relevant to modern brewing.

The idea to use pasteurization to eliminate unwanted microorganisms at the end of fermentation came from Pasteur. Obviously, Pasteur's contribution to the standardization of the finished product was only the beginning for the large-scale production of beer. The industrial revolution brought many other important developments. In 1883, in the Carlsberg laboratory in Copenhagen, Denmark, Emil Hansen became the first person to isolate and multiply a single pure yeast cell. He used the yeast to make Lager, and he classified the yeast species as *Unterhefe Nr. I* (bottom-fermenting yeast 1). The Fahrenheit thermometer and Benjamin Martin's saccharometer allowed brewers to measure the amount of sugar in their mashes, which helped them to more accurately determine when the fermentation process was complete. The Watt steam engine, developed in 1765, was also a fundamental contribution, as it allowed brewers to crush malt at much faster rates. At the beginning of the 19th century, Daniel Wheeler invented a device to kiln and roast malt. The German scientist Carl Von Linde developed the first refrigerators, which allowed breweries to store large quantities of ingredients and better control beer temperatures during the fermentation process. At the end of the century, the mass-production of the glass bottle gave brewers the ideal delivery system for getting their beers into the hands of customers.

The 20th Century

After World Wars I and II, local breweries began disappearing. Financial crises and political turmoil increased the demand for cheap, mass-produced goods. Huge brewing conglomerates emerged that could take advantage of industrialization and globalization to sell their products overseas. They sourced ingredients and labor from different countries to cut down on costs. Beer-making became less of a craft and more of an industrial puzzle. In the UK, the organization CAMRA (the Campaign for Real Ale) was founded in 1971, with the goal of rediscovering traditional forms of English brewing. The term "Real Ale" wasn't meant to identify any particular style of beer, but rather to distinguish certain types of cask beers made using live yeast instead of instant yeast. These ales were often brewed by local pubs and pumped directly from the cask.

However, the true beer revolution began in the United States, when homebrewing made a powerful comeback in the 1970s. The passion and desire to rediscover long-forgotten brewing practices led many brewers to travel around Europe studying beer production. Beer-centric countries such as Belgium, Germany, and England were fountains of lost beer knowledge. Upon returning to the United States, brewers set to work combining what they had learned overseas with modern brewing techniques. Thanks to the passion of people like Charlie Papazian—the "father of homebrewing" and founder of the American Homebrewers Association—the world was ready for a beer renaissance.

Geography

Spain played an important role in the production of beer during the Roman Empire, but over time it ceded much of its beer reputation to Germany. France, thanks to Pasteur's discoveries, has managed to earn a place in beer history despite its clear preference for wine. Italy is also known as a wine powerhouse, but recently it has nurtured a growing craft brew scene. Many other countries around the world have contributed to beer production, but in general four macro-regions of beer have emerged, which we have lumped into geographical areas for convenience: Germany, Belgium, the UK and Ireland, and the United States. Although the real picture is actually much broader, these four macro-regions and their brewing traditions are largely responsible for developing the styles of beer we enjoy today.

Germany

Germany's brewing tradition can be traced back to the nomadic populations that inhabited the region thousands of years ago. These cultures didn't leave written records of their brewing techniques, but we know that by the second century, they were trading the beer they produced with neighboring peoples.

Bavarian beers are a great place to start. There's Helles, a bottom-fermented beer and a masterpiece of simplicity; Weizenbier, a top-fermented wheat beer with a phenolic character achieved through the yeast used; Radler (Shandy), a Pils or Lager mixed with lemonade; and Kellerbier (cellar beer), which is traditionally aged in cellars and bottled unfiltered.

In Cologne, they produce a top-fermented Golden Ale called Kölsch. This style, which has been granted Protected Geographical Indication (PGI) by the European Union, is a huge part of Cologne's culture and one of its major exports.

Breweries in Düsseldorf produce Altbier, another top-fermented beer. This one has a darker color due to the roasted malt used in its production.

In Bamberg, they make Rauchbier, a bottom-fermented beer brewed with smoked malts. It is now common practice for the malt used in Rauchbier to be smoked over a beechwood fire, inspired by the methods of Bamberg's only two breweries (Schlenkerla and Spezial), which have been producing this beer for centuries. Gose is another beer style that contains very specific ingredients. In this case, the product isn't characterized by the way the malt barley is processed, but rather by the water used to make it. This Lager, which is typical of Leipzig and has its origins in medieval Goslar, is famous for the presence of salt in the water used to make it, as well as for the significant quantities of wheat and spices present in the brew. The resulting beer is salty, spicy, and sour—a strange combination achievable through the addition of lactic acid bacteria. The use of this bacteria was only recently rediscovered, after having fallen by the wayside during much of the 20th century. Berlin, on the other hand, is famous for its Berliner Weisse (white beer), which is often made with raspberry syrup or woodruff to balance out its acidity. This fresh, low-alcohol beer, which doesn't have a strict percentage of wheat, was very popular in Berlin throughout the 19th century. It fell out of fashion during the 20th century, as the breweries that made it couldn't compete with commercial breweries. The curiosity of young brewers all over the world has led to the rediscovery and reinterpretation of this unique style.

Belgium

For such a small country, Belgium has a complicated past full of revolutions, secessions, annexations, cultural and political transformations, and internal conflicts. Perhaps this is why it has cultivated such a wide variety of beer styles.

When we think of Belgian beers, we immediately think of Trappist beers, which can be identified by their famous hexagonal logo. "Trappist" isn't actually a style of beer, but rather a controlled beer production method. Six Trappist monasteries in Belgium use this method to make beer. Belgium also produces Sours like Red Flemish Ale and Lambic (a spontaneously fermented beer), high ABV beers such as Tripel and Quadrupel, session beers like Wit beer, and numerous spiced beers and hop beers. Its many Lagers are also famous throughout the world. How do so many different styles coexist within such a small country? Adherence to tradition on the part of Belgian brewers is certainly part of the answer, but the rediscovery of many lost Belgian brews has come about largely because of American brewers who, in the 1980s and 90s, gradually abandoned British influences and started to explore the beer traditions of Belgium.

Today, thanks to America's newfound interest in Belgian brewing, Belgian beer production is flourishing once again, and many breweries throughout the world are now producing Belgian-inspired beers.

The UK and Ireland

The brewing traditions of the British Isles are just as culturally rich as those of Germany and Belgium. The British were already drinking beer when the Romans arrived, although the practice wasn't widespread. By the 4th century, the Anglo Saxons introduced new brewing techniques. Women were chiefly responsible for brewing beer at this time, as it could be done at home. Indeed, many women became master brewers, and some even began serving beer in their houses to paying customers. This practice led to the birth of ale houses, the true ancestors of pubs and bars. Taxes and tighter regulations soon followed, as local regions wanted to ensure the quality of the beer produced and combat public drunkenness. Beer licenses came after that, leading to the development of ale houses (which typically served only beer), taverns (which also served food, wine, and spirits), and inns (where travelers could also stay the night). In an official document issued by Henry III in the 13th century, corporal punishments were established to prevent the illegal brewing or selling of beer. The document uses the term "brewster" (a medieval term for a female brewer), which alerts us to the fact that women were still the driving force behind beer at that time.

The beer trade became increasingly important (and lucrative), and ale houses remained in vogue until the end of the 17th century. From the 18th century onward (and following the industrial revolution), ale houses were gradually replaced by the Victorian public house, or pub, which has become a symbol of the UK and a big part of its culture. Local brewing became too costly and cumbersome, as larger brewers could sell beers at much lower prices. Porter is one of the most famous beers of this era. Traditionally, Porter was a blend of older beer with new beer. It got its name from the "porters" who worked in the London markets delivering goods to businesses and customers.

In Ireland, Arthur Guinness is credited with developing a recipe for a more intense version of Porter, called Extra Stout Porter, which was later perfected by his son (also named Arthur). In the UK, Porter beers suffered a sharp decline during the 19th and 20th centuries. Pale Ales began to take over the market, while the appearance of the IPA all but eclipsed the Porter.

Following World War II, the world fell in love with Lagers, but this trend was slow to reach the British Isles. Due to economic factors and national pride, the market for bottom-fermented blond beers didn't develop there until the 1970s. By then, Lagers slowly began to crowd out other varieties of beer in pubs, leading to the gradual decline of many traditional British beers. However, some of these beers have been rediscovered by CAMRA and by waves of new American brewers, who have also experimented with them to create their own styles.

Today, the British brewing scene is alive and well, mixing traditional styles with innovative new techniques. Each year, breweries around the world look to the UK and Ireland for liquid inspiration.

The United States

Although a young country, the United States has had a massive impact on beer production, especially in recent years. After the first Europeans settled in the New World, breweries began to pop up along the East Coast (especially in New York City, Philadelphia, and Baltimore). These breweries were mostly run by Dutch brewers (when New York was still New Amsterdam) and British-born Americans. For political and economic reasons, the beer industry in America remained stagnant until after the American Revolutionary War. Following the war, the production of Porters, Pale Ales, and IPAs exploded, especially in the eastern United States. Things changed radically in the mid-19th century, when waves of German immigrants arrived. Lager began to take over beer menus across the country. Almost every city in the United States, from the east coast to the west coast, had a local brewery serving bottom-fermented beers. Many of these beers had rice or maize in their brews to lighten their colors. Although beer production increased rapidly in large metropolises, the true revolution occurred in the Midwest, where breweries focused on technological innovations and beer standardization. Miller Brewing Co. in Milwaukee and Anheuser Busch in St. Louis began to dominate the industry. But the 20th century saw the implementation of Prohibition. Many breweries were forced to close their doors, as Prohibitionists argued that alcohol was the root of many of the country's problems, including politcal turmoil, family violence, and poverty.

Prior to Prohibition, there were roughly 1,200 breweries in the United States. By 1935, there were just over 700. During the postwar economic boom, beer consumption in the United States steadily increased, but breweries—hindered by restrictive laws and the monopolization of a few large brands—continued to struggle to stay open. In 1978, there were only 89 breweries operating in the country, most of them controlled by large groups.

The "American Beer Renaissance" didn't begin until the 1970s. In 1965, the Anchor Brewing Company was purchased by Fritz Maytag. Rather than conforming to current brewing trends, he decided to continue producing classic beer styles, such as the Steam Beer. In 1976, Jack McAuliffe founded the New Albion Brewery in Sonoma, California. This is viewed as a pivotal moment in the revival of beer. Albeit a short-lived experiment (6 years), the New Albion Brewery inspired legions of homebrewers and small-business breweries.

Brewery numbers slowly began to trend upwards once again. By 2011, there were over 2,000 breweries in the United States. By 2018, the number had reached 7,450—almost double the previous high-point of American brewing, which occured in 1873, when there were roughly 4,173 breweries in operation.

Production

Beer is an alcoholic drink because of the yeast used in its fermentation process, though there are also many nonalcoholic beers on the market today!

It is generally made with cereal grains, including malted barley, wheat, oats, rye, sorghum, and millet. It can also be produced with potatoes, which are rich in starch! Brewers have become increasingly focused on the aromatics of beer. Fresh hops add a spicy, herbal aroma, but many other essences continue to be experimented with in beer, including pepper, citrus, bread, raisins, chocolate, pine, grasses, toffee, and bananas. Water is also an essential ingredient in beer, as the grain seeds need moisture in order to germinate.

We can thus loosely define beer as a product of alcoholic fermentation created via the brewing of cereal grains. Malted barley is the most common cereal grain used in the brewing process, though wheat, maize, and rice are also used. The unfermented mixture is called the "sweet wort." The wort must be boiled, as this sterilizes the liquid and stops the starch from converting into sugar. The hops are then added in batches for flavoring. After the resulting mixture has cooled, the yeast is introduced. Now the mixure is ready to ferment and become beer.

The Main ingredients

Water

Water is the most important ingredient in beer. Beer simply can't exist without water. Different types of water sourced from different locations around the globe can subtly influence beer quality. Certain beers require specific types of water with strict chemical characteristics. For example, certain Porters benefit from water with high levels of bicarbonate, while certain Pilsners require water with lower levels of bicarbonate.

Yeasts

According to accomplished homebrewer Dave Miller, "Brewers make the wort, but yeast makes the beer." Yeast is the microorganism that is responsible for fermentation in beer. It metabolises the sugars extracted from grains, which makes alcohol and carbon dioxide, thereby turning the wort into beer. The main forms of yeast used to make beer are *Saccharomyces cervisiae,* known as Ale yeast, and *Saccharomyces pastorianus,* known as Lager yeast.

The etymology of the word *Saccharomyces* tells us a lot about yeast. It's a mold (*-myces*) that "likes" sugar (*saccharo*). Yeast cells are in fact able to "eat" sugars and produce ethyl alcohol and carbon dioxide through a completely natural and physiological process. Before the role of yeast in fermentation was discovered, fermentation involved wild or airborne yeasts.

Saccharomyces cerevisiae are also called "top-fermenting" yeasts. They work at higher temperatures (between about 60-77 °F/15-25 °C) near the surface of the vats, where they create a foam. These yeasts give life to all "top-fermented" beers, such as Ales.

Saccharomyces pastorianus are also called "bottom-fermenting" yeasts, as they work at lower temperatures (below 54 °F/12 °C) and at the "bottom" of the vats. Beers produced with these yeasts are called "low- fermented" beers and include Lagers.

Malted Barley and Other Cereal Grains

After water, malted barley, or malt, is the most important ingredient in the production of beer.

The barley is converted into malt through a process known as "malting." This process allows the brewer to control the beer's color, aroma, and taste. The sugars of the wort, and consequently the alcoholic strength and body of the beer, are determined by the malt, which is very rich in starch.

During malting, barley seeds are steeped in water to kick off the germinating process. This activates a series of enzymes that open up the seeds' energy reserves (starch), which leads them to germinate. These precious enzymes are the brewer's ally in the preparation of the wort and the saccharification of starch. The germinated seeds are then dried, preventing the growth of seedlings or rootlets. Many different types of malts can be created depending on the temperatures used during the malting process and the amount of time the seeds are steeped in water, and every malt has its own unique characteristics.

Hops

Hops give beer its characteristic bitterness. They can also add floral, fruity, and citrus flavors and aromas. The quality of a batch of hops depends on its soil and growing region. Hops have antiseptic and antioxidant properties, which makes them a natural preservative. The hop tree is a climbing plant that grows spontaneously in temperate regions both north and south of the equator. Hops have become increasingly important to the brewing process over the years.

The female flowers, or strobuli, are often called cones. They contain the acids and essential oils that impart aroma and bitterness to beer. The flowers produce lupulin, a sticky, yellow powder that contains resins and the oils. There are many varieties of hops, each with specific characteristics that help define different beer profiles, just like grapes in wine. Some hops are added more for the aromas they impart, while others are added more for their bitterness. "Old World" hops, also sometimes called "noble" hops, have been cultivated in Europe for thousands of years and are used in many classic beers. These hop varieties include Saaz, Hallertauer, Tettnanger, and Spalt. The flavors they impart are considered more subtle. Many American hop varieties, in contrast, aren't subtle at all. They are known for being bright, citrusy, and resinous.

Other Ingredients

In the world's diverse beerscape, it's not unusual to encounter unique ingredients, such as honey, ginger, coffee, fruit (cherries, raspberries, figs, chestnuts), spices (pepper, coriander, cinnamon, vanilla), or roots (licorice, gentian). While some of these ingredients are part of regional or historical traditions, others are the result of painstaking experimentation and research.

The Brewing Process

The brewing process seeks to achieve two basic things. The first is to obtain wort sugars from the cereal grains. The second is to produce ethyl alcohol and carbon dioxide from these sugars, which happens after the yeast is added and the mixture ferments. The sugars, mostly maltose, are produced as malted barley converts to starch.

Saccharification occurs when enzymes are activated during the first stage of the mashing process, which is when the ground malt is mixed with hot water. This stage usually lasts around 2 hours.

During this first stage, it is important for the mixture to have the correct grain-to-gallon ratio. Its pH and temperature must be closely monitored. This is the moment in which the brewer chooses which malts to use and how the malts should be proportioned. They must also determine the saccharification temperature needed to produce the variety of beer they are hoping to make. The types of malt will determine the beer's color, flavor, and basic aroma, whereas the mashing temperature will influence saccharification, the beer's body, and it's final alcohol content.

Mash tuns in a brewery. They are used for mixing the ground malt (grist) with temperature-controlled water.

The next stage is filtration, a process in which solids, such as the husks of the barley kernels, are removed from the wort to obtain a clear liquid, which is then transferred to the brew kettle to be boiled. The wort is then enriched with hops and boiled for 1-2 hours. This will help sterilize it and concentrate its sugars to the desired level.

Once boiled, it is possible to add more hops to the wort to boost its flavor. The hops and the hot break (the proteins that coagulate during boiling) are then separated by centrifugal force in a whirlpool vessel. The wort is then cooled down to fermentation temperature, oxygenated, and transferred to vats, where it will mix with the yeast that will ferment it and convert it into beer. After 5-10 days of fermentation, the beer undergoes a longer sedimentation and maturation process. For Lagers, this can last many weeks.

The last stage is packaging. Beer can be transferred to bottles, cans, recyclable stainless-steel kegs, or disposable plastic kegs. There is one great distinction present at this stage: brewers can opt for pasteurization or microfiltration, or skip these steps entirely and go straight to bottling.

Filled beer bottles on a conveyor belt.

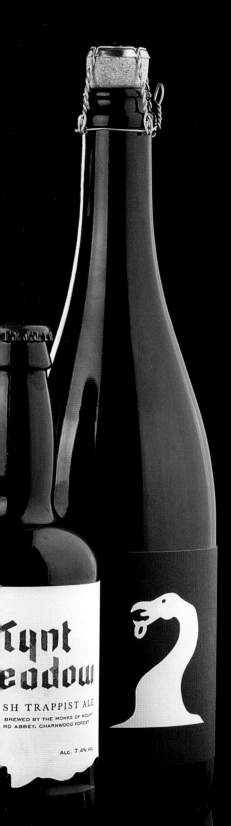

The Many Styles of Beer

There are an untold number of beer styles in the world today. This is due to beer's rich history, the seemingly limitless supply of ingredients that can be used to make it, its spread to so many diverse countries, and a growing interest in brewing methods and experimentation. It takes time for new beer styles to be documented, as they first have to catch on and earn more recognition before their characteristics can be explored and replicated by other brewers.

There is no such thing as an official, universally recognized categorization system for beer styles. They are divided into groups and sub-groups based on certain characteristics that unite or distinguish them: color, alcohol content, ingredients, brewing technique, historical origins, and region. Although these factors are important, there are numerous beers with characteristics that don't fit neatly into established categories. There are also beers that are nearly identical in composition but that still wind up in separate categories due to a few small details. Of course, in our opinion, the sensory experience of drinking a beer is critical to determining how it should be categorized. Appearance, aroma, taste, and texture are usually the points that matter most to those interested in broadening their beer horizons. The most complete attempt at the categorization of the sensory profiles of beer styles is most likely BJCP's "Beer Style Guidelines." The Beer Judge Certificate Program, a nonprofit organization established in 1985 in the United States, promotes beer culture and trains beer judges for beer competitions. BJCP's guidelines were used as a reference while compiling the beer style information in this book.

It must be noted that beer is actually less regulated than many other food products, which contributes to the complexity and confusion in trying to categorize its styles.

If we order a wine like Brunello di Montalcino, certain key characteristics will be present. The wine will have a specific color, a specific alcohol content, and a specific sensory profile. This is because the wine is produced according to a legally recognized product specification, which holds that it can only be made with a specific grape variety grown in a specific area and matured in wooden barrels for a specific length of time.

But when we order a Pilsner, a Lager that derives its name from the Czech city of Pilsen, where it was first produced, do we know exactly what we're getting? Not at all! The term "Pilsner" has never belonged solely to any company or organization, and therefore any brewery in the world can produce its own version of a Pilsner and market it as such. And while they're brewing it, they don't necessarily have to use Lager yeasts, Moravian malts, or Saaz (a noble Bohemian hop variety), which are some of the normal Pilsner ingredients. The beer they produce may wind up with a very different profile than a traditional, golden-yellow, bottom-fermented Pilsner.

So, craft beer newbies should be aware that the world of beer isn't lacking in contradictions. Understanding beer requires a certain amount of mental flexibility! We hope that the following 14 beer groups arm you with a little more beer knowledge as you take your growler out to new breweries, bars, and pubs. As beer styles continue to evolve, understanding the sensory side of beer will help you appreciate and share your knowledge and enthusiasm for the beverage of beer.

Keller and Helles: Traditional Bavarian Bottom-fermented Pale Lagers

These Lagers are the prototypes for light beers the world over. They are among the most popular, most imitated, and most revolutionized beers on the market, and yet somehow they're still often underrated, as many people consider them too traditional to excite their taste buds. Traditional, certainly, but the best ones are never boring!

They tend to be pale, though they sometimes have faint amber colors. They are usually light countryside beers hovering around 5% alcohol and made with local ingredients. The sweet, honey-like taste of pale malts hits the palate first, then the delicate bitterness of the hops, and finally the subtle, yeasty edge, which is usually due to the yeasts being deliberately left in the beer. They are produced with respect to centuries-old recipes, with little room for interpretation on the part of master brewers. Many local brewers in Bavaria still make them in their cellars. They are also made by large breweries, which export them all over the world in bottles and kegs. They emerged as a result of the technological innovations of the first industrial revolution. During that time, lightly roasted malts were being produced, which allowed for paler beers. In short, the beers in this category glow like gold and taste like sunshine. What's not to love?

UNGESPUNDET
NATURTRÜB

"aU" Ungespundet Naturtrüb

Style: *KELLERBIER*

ABV: *5.2%*
Fermentation: *Bottom*
Bottle: *17 fl oz (0.5 l) with a crown cap*

Producer: *Mahrs Brau*
Locality: *Bamberg*
(Upper Franconia – Germany)

Mahrs Brau is a centuries-old brewery that has been in the skilled hands of the same brewery dynasty, the Michel family, since 1895. They brew their beers with great respect for the past and for the environment. At the same time, they've kept up with innovation and technological advancements.

The *Ungespundet* part of this beer's name means "unbunged." This refers to the beer's traditional maturation process, during which it was left in "unbunged" (open) barrels so that a certain amount of carbon dioxide could escape. The result is a beer with a much gentler level of carbonation. Unfiltered beers belong to the large Kellerbier family. They were once brewed and stored in cool underground cellars and served directly to customers in beer gardens. In the Mahrs Biergarten, you'll still find *aU* (pronounced "ah-ooh") served from traditional wooden barrels.

Profile

Appearance: *bright amber color, with a light beige head*
Aroma: *richly honeyish, malty, and herbaceous, with pungent, yeasty notes*
Mouthfeel: *a delicate dryness softens the richness of the malt and brings out a pleasant, hoppy bitterness; the finishing notes have a citrus edge, which accentuates its sharpness*
Overall Impression: *a straightforward yet interesting beer that offers a touch of complexity without being too heavy*

Zoigl

Style: *KELLERBIER*

ABV: *5%* **Producer:** *Klosterbrauerei Mallersdorf*
Fermentation: *Bottom* **Locality:** *Mallersdorf-Pfaffenberg*
Bottle: *17 fl oz (0.5 l) with a flip-top* *(Lower Bavaria – Germany)*

The Zoigl featured here is produced by the Poor Franciscan Sisters of the Holy Family in Mallersdorf-Pfaffenberg, Germany. The brewery is run by the hardworking and hospitable Sister Doris (the last surviving nun-brewmistress in Europe), while Sister Regelinde handles the commercial side and oversees the on-site shop. The honest spirit of this abbey and its beer is perhaps best embodied in the face of Sister Doris on the label. The abbey's nearby guesthouse has a beer garden that's well worth a visit. They also carry a selection of seasonal products from their vegetable gardens.

Zoigl is a light, unfiltered Lager (*mit Hefe* translates to "with yeast") that concentrates more on malts than hops. It also boasts a rich history. The term "zoigl" refers to a brewing tradition of the Upper Palatinate, where beer was only brewed in communal brewhouses overseen by several authorized families. The beer they made was then matured in cellars, with each family putting its own spin on how their beer was blended. The families were identified by a sign (*zoigl* in dialect), which was attached to their houses: a six-pointed brewer's star.

Profile
Appearance: *deep golden color, slightly hazy, with a persistent, frothy white head*
Aroma: *honey and cereal grains, with notes of freshly baked bread*
Mouthfeel: *dominated by a malty sweetness, with a rounded body*
Overall Impression: *simple, balanced, rustic, and extremely drinkable*

Fischerin Vom Bodensee

Style: *HELLES BIER*

ABV: *4.8%* **Producer:** *Ruppaner Privatbrauerei*
Fermentation: *Bottom* **Locality:** *Konstanz*
Bottle: *11 fl oz (0.33 l) with a crown cap* *(Baden-Württemberg – Germany)*

The independent brewery featured here is situated on the shores of Lake Constance in southern Germany, on the border with Switzerland. It also happens to be closely located to one of the oldest settlements to ever brew beer, the Abbey of Saint Gall. The brewery was founded in 1795 and has been owned by the Ruppaner family since 1872. It's a classic example of traditional Teutonic brewing culture, focusing on the use of local high-quality ingredients, paying constant tribute to its glorious past, and ensuring that many traditional styles continue to live on. The label proudly references Bavaria's legendary Purity Law of 1516, issued by Duke William IV of Bavaria.

Fischerin vom Bodensee Helles is an extremely drinkable light beer. It's perfect for those summer afternoons spent drinking a few beers with friends, or when you're relaxing by a lake in a comfortable chair, daydreaming of all the breweries you'd like to visit.

Profile
Appearance: *clear, light-gold color, with a compact, white head*
Aroma: *delicate malty notes with hints of acacia honey*
Mouthfeel: *thin, smooth body with a vibrant effervescence that supports the prevailing sweet taste of pale malts; this is followed by a touch of hoppy bitterness*
Overall Impression: *a simple and instantly gratifying beer with a wildly enjoyable light taste*

Other Lagers

Three different styles of Lager—with very little in common—are presented in this group to offer a broader view of this huge family of diverse beers.

The first false myth to dispel is that not all Lagers are clear: Dunkel, Schwarz, Bock, and Doppelbock are all Lager styles that use caramel and dark malts to obtain a color that can range from dark amber to brown to pitch black. Another common misconception is that Lagers are light beers: they're not. Lagers often have double-digit alcohol contents, light and dark alike. To help illustrate these two lesser-known aspects of Lagers, we've included a very classic Dopplebock from the oldest continuously operating brewery in the world, the Weihenstephan Brewery in Germany.

For those who believe that Lagers can't be bitter, take a look at the Pilsner (also called Pilsener, Pilsen, or simply Pils), a Lager style created in the Bohemian city of Pilsen in 1842, when pale beers were all the rage. This Pale Lager stands out from the others due to its bitterness and more distinctive hop taste. Indeed, the Pilsner is credited with introducing hops to the Lager and adding a new dimension to its bold flavor profile.

Finally, the last style in this group is one that has fallen a little out of fashion recently: the Export Lager.

Tipopils

Style: *KELLERPILS*

ABV: *5.2%*

Producer: *Birrificio*

entation: *Bottom*

Locality: *Limido Co*

with a crown cap

(Lombardy – Italy)

ne of the pioneers of the Italian cr
en its flagship beer ever since its
brewery's founder and master bre
wanted to put qualitative growth
anted to take the traditional Pale L
al taste, which he did with Tipopils
roughly to "kind of"), this is not a tr
German Pils. Instead, it's a kind-of
e fact that it isn't microfiltered. Thi
r style. Arioli dry-hops Central Eur
hich enhances the beer's aroma, tas
e beer first appeared, German and
source of the hops used, confusing t

ving numerous awards in compe
also been confirmed by its popula
orldwide have launched imitation
has led to the birth of another sub-s

Profile

Edelstoff

Style: *GERMAN HELLES EXPORTBIER*

ABV: *5.6%*
Fermentation: *Bottom*
Bottle: *17 fl oz (0.5 l) with a crown cap*

Producer: *Augustiner-Brau Wagner KG*
Locality: *Munich*
(Bavaria – Germany)

Augustiner beer was created in 1328 by Augustinian monks in Munich, Germany. Augustinian monks produced it for centuries, until their monastery closed in the early 1800s. The brewery became state-owned and continued to function, but it was eventually privatized and purchased by the Wagner family. The letters JW on the label stand for the initials of Joseph Wagner. In 2013, the brewery opened the Augustiner Klosterwirt restaurant on the site of the monastery where the beer was first brewed. Augustiner is one of the six official breweries that provide beer for Munich's Oktoberfest, but it's the only one that serves its beer directly from wooden barrels during the festivities. It's also the only brewery of the six that does its own malting.

Edelstoff Exportbier was launched in 1925. It was introduced as a noble (*edel*) beer and has a fairly strict list of ingredients. In German tradition, the term "Export" originally referred to strong beers produced in Dortmund, many of which were meant to be exported. The term now refers to slightly stronger light beers in general, including beers not intended for export.

Profile

Appearance: *straw-yellow color, with a medium, white head*
Aroma: *pale malt and acacia honey, herbaceous, with a hint of noble hops*
Mouthfeel: *smooth, medium body; malty sweetness; a little mineraly, with a touch of bitterness in the finish*
Overall Impression: *good overall balance and a thicker, malty character*

Korbinian

Style: *DOPPELBOCK*

ABV: *7.4%*
Fermentation: *Bottom*
Bottle: *17 fl oz (0.5 l) with a crown cap*
Producer: *Bayerische Staatsbrauerei*

Weihenstephan (Bavarian State
Brewery Weihenstephan)
Locality: *Weihenstephan*
(Freising – Bavaria – Germany)

This beer boasts a long history. It bears the name of Saint Korbinian, a monk who arrived in Freising around 720 AD and founded the Church of Saint Stephen, which later became the Benedictine monastery of the same name. It was here that the Weihenstephan brewery was established in 1040, licensed by the City of Freising. However, there is evidence that the monks first began brewing beer at the monastery as early as the end of the 8th century. Production of this monastic beer was interrupted in the early 1800s, when the monastery was confiscated by the state.

It was secularized in 1923, and the brewery was given its current name, the Weihenstephan State Brewery (*Bayerische Staatsbrauerei Weihenstephan*). It was run in collaboration with the University of Munich, eventually becoming an intellectual and artistic hub. Traditionally, the monks produced Doppelbocks for sustenance. They were much sweeter, less alcoholic, and more full-bodied than they typically are today, hence the nickname "liquid bread."

Korbinian is one of the few Doppelbocks with a name that doesn't end in "-ator," which comes from its progenitor "Salvator," brewed by Paulaner monks in Munich. Korbinian remains an elegant and modern beer.

Profile
Appearance: *mahogany color with copper highlights; clear,*
with a thin and persistent dark-beige head
Aroma: *dark malt and caramel, mild fruity aromas of plum, fig, and roasted hazelnut*
Mouthfeel: *medium-full body, medium-low carbonation;*
sweet notes balanced by a delicate roastiness
Overall Impression: *a triumph of malts; smooth, strong, rich; it slides across*
the tongue but lingers long enough for the taste to burst through

"Classic" Trappist Beer

"Trappist" beer generally refers to beer produced inside an abbey of monks belonging to the Order of Cistercians of the Strict Observance (Latin: *Ordo Cisterciensis Strictioris Observantiae*). The monks are called Trappist in honor of the Cistercian abbey of La Trappe in Soligny, Normandy (France), where the order was founded in 1664. The aim of the order was to return to the strict observance of the original Rule of Saint Benedict, which resulted in a more contemplative and austere environment. This reform renewed the practices of silence, manual labor, and suppressed recreational activities. Further, monks couldn't eat or drink with the community outside of their abbey. This last dictate gradually fell out of favor, as the monks began producing beer and selling it far and wide. Although the Trappists are primarily dedicated to work, prayer, and study, their brewing skills are unparalleled. Surprisingly, making beer isn't even one of their main activities. The International Trappist Association (ITA) was established in 1997 with the aim of recognizing and protecting all "Authentic Trappist Products" (cheese, beer, biscuits, jam, etc.) with an official hexagonal logo. Only 7 monasteries out of more than 150 produce beer. The phrase "Old Trappists" refers to beers made by the original group of Belgium Trappists that founded the above association (this group's brewing traditions are much older). The "Modern Trappists" are a more recent group (established in 2012) and have abbeys all over the world.

Westmalle Tripel

Style: *TRIPEL*

ABV: *9.5%*
Fermentation: *Top*
Bottle: *25 fl oz (0.75 l) with a mushroom cork*

Producer: *The Trappists of the Abbey of Our Lady of the Sacred Heart of Westmalle*
Locality: *Malle (Antwerp – Belgium)*

The first monastery in Westmalle, Belgium, was founded in 1794 by Trappist monks fleeing La Trappe in France. During the French Revolution, monasteries and other religious properties were confiscated by the government, forcing many monks into exile. In 1836, after years of uncertainty and difficulty, the order establishd a small brewery to make beer for the monks living in the monastery. However, when they began selling their beer in surroundings towns, it surged in popularity. Since 1861, the beers brewed at Westmalle Brewery have ensured the monastery's economic stability.

The most important Westmalle beer is the Tripel, a precursor to many modern-day strong pale ales. The Tripel was created in 1938 under the name Superbier. It's a lighter beer with a high alcohol content. In the 1950s, more hops were added to the recipe and the name was changed to Tripel. Many consider this beer deceptive, as it's so smooth and refreshing that the high alcohol content is well-masked. It's often made with pale candy sugar and has a sunny color resulting from a mash of pilsener malts. The hops are Styrian Goldings, sometimes mixed with other German varieties. The Tripel is beloved by brewers everywhere, and many of them still use it today as a stylistic reference point.

Profile

Appearance: *clear, golden yellow (with yeast sediment); an exuberant and very persistent white head*

Aroma: *fruit (fresh, ripe, jammy), flowers, spices, shortbread; herbaceous, ethery*

Mouthfeel: *the sweetness of malt is mitigated by the beer's light body, dryness, effervescence, and bitter finish*

Overall Impression: *the product of an incredible yeast, this beer is sure to delight all who taste it*

CHIMAY

PERES TRAPPISTES

GRANDE RÉSERVE
VIEILLIE EN BARRIQUES

WOOD TYPES: *French oak, american oak, rum*
ALCOHOL: 10,5% vol. | BOTTLING DATE: 15/02/2017
3 FERMENTATIONS: *Tank, Barrel, Bottle*

Chimay
Grande Réserve Vieillie En Barriques 2017

Style: *BELGIAN STRONG DARK ALE, BARREL-AGED*

ABV: *10.5%*
Fermentation: *Top*
Bottle: *25 fl oz (0.75 l) with a mushroom cork*

Producer: *The Trappists of the Abbey of Our Lady in Scourmont*
Locality: *Chimay (Hainaut – Belgium)*

The history of Scourmont Abbey begins in 1850, when a few Trappist monks from Westvleteren Abbey (where beer was already being produced) arrived at a poor sharecropper's farm. Though the farm was surrounded by muddy swamps and wild forests, it was eventually transformed into a thriving cheese dairy and brewery. In 1862, the monks of Chimay drank their first home-brewed beer, and in 1864 they began selling their beer outside the monastery to finance their charitable works.

Today, Chimay produces more beer than any other Trappist brewery. While financial growth is certainly important to the abbey, the brewery's mainstay products have remained at only four. Featured here is a special edition of the iconic Chimay Blue, the monastery's flagship beer. It was first brewed in 1956 as a Christmas beer.

This barrique-aged Grande Réserve Vieillie En Barriques is a good symbol of Trappist quality, which favors tradition and taste over innovation. Each beer they make reflects the values, craftsmanship, and dedication of the monks who've tended to their unique recipes for generations.

Profile

Appearance: *brown color with coppery highlights and a thick, creamy, off-white head*
Aroma: *caramel, toffee, vanilla, marzipan; a touch of coffee, spirit-soaked fruit, wood, cognac, and rum*
Mouthfeel: *light, yet velvety body, delicate tannins, sweet; roasted malt, raisins, hints of rum*
Overall Impression: *best opened at least one year after bottling, as this allows its distinct flavors to balance out*

Orval

Style: *BELGIAN SPECIALITY ALE*

ABV: *6.2%*
Fermentation: *Mixed*
(Top + Brettanomyces)
Bottle: *11 fl oz (0.33 l) with a crown cap*

Producer: *The Trappists of the Abbey of Our Lady in Orval*
Locality: *Villers-devant-Orval (Luxemburg – Belgium)*

Orval Abbey is legendary in the world of beer-making. Its fascinating history begins in the 11th century. Italian Benedictine monks built its first church and monastery, though eventually these fell into the hands of French Cistercians. In the 1900s, Trappist monk Marie-Albert van der Cruyssen took over its direction and oversaw its restoration. The widowed countess Matilda of Tuscany is believed to have lost her wedding ring in a nearby spring. According to legend, she prayed for its return, and her prayers were answered when a trout burst out of the water with her ring in its mouth. The countess exclaimed: "This place is truly a Val d'Or!" (valley of gold). Sadly, this legend wasn't enough to save the abbey from destruction at the hands of the French Revolutionary Army. The old abbey remained in ruins from the end of the 1700s until 1926, when it was returned to the Trappists, who brought it back to life. The brewery was established to help finance its reconstruction. Its operations are supervised by monks, but many responsibilities are entrusted to professional laypeople. A single master beer recipe was created from scratch, and this recipes is still in use today. Orval Brewery was the first Trappist brewery to distribute its beer nationally. Its logo depicts a trout with a golden ring in its mouth—a tribute to Matilda of Tuscany. The brewery makes one beer and one beer only, but why mess with perfection?

Profile

Appearance: *light, hazy amber color; frothy white head with moderate persistence*
Aroma: *peppery, herbaceous; yellow plum, orange zest*
Mouthfeel: *medium-light body, very effervescent; licorice, rhubarb, dry, fruity, spicy*
Overall Impression: *fresh and thirst-quenching, but also with a rich aftertaste and a lingering aroma*

"Modern" Trappist Beer

For years, we were accustomed to the same Trappist monasteries brewing the same consistent (and excellent) beers: Chimay, Orval, Rochefort, Westmalle, and Westvleteren in Belgium, and Koningshoeven in the Netherlands. The latest addition was Achel Abbey, again in Belgium, which started brewing in 1998.

Then suddenly, in 2012, a new age of Modern Trappists began: in less than 8 years, five new breweries have popped up around the world, offering many innovative products:

• *Stift Engelszell* (2012, Austria), which focuses on Weizenbier and uses imaginative names for its beers.

• *Maria Toevlucht "Zundert"* (2013, the Netherlands), the most like the Old Trappists.

• *Spencer Brewery at St. Joseph's Abbey* (2014, USA), the first Trappist monastery outside Europe, and possibly the most creative. It makes canned IPAs, Imperial Stout, and fruit beers.

• *Abbey of the Tre Fontane in Rome* (2015, Italy), which uses many unique ingredients, including eucalyptus.

• *Mount St. Bernard Abbey "Tynt Meadow"* (2018, UK), known for its wonderful English Strong Ale.

Will the Modern Trappists be able to match the success of their predecessors? Will the growth of Trappist breweries generate more interest or more confusion among enthusiasts? Will they boost the already-stellar image of Trappist beers? Only time will tell. For now, we'll have to be content with tasting them all and judging for ourselves.

Spencer Trappist Imperial Stout

Style: *IMPERIAL STOUT*

ABV: *8.7%*
Fermentation: *Top*
Bottle: *11 fl oz (0.33 l) with a crown cap*

Producer: *The Trappists of St. Joseph's Abbey in Spencer*
Locality: *Spencer (Massachussets – USA)*

The Trappists came to the United States from France in the early 1800s, driven, as always, by the need to escape chaotic European political events. The first settlement in Nova Scotia in 1825 is closely linked to the Trappists in Spencer, Massachusetts. The abbey dates back to 1950 and mainly made jams and jellies to support itself. A beer enthusiast and homebrewer entered the community, and he drew their attention to brewing, which other Trappist abbeys had already been perfecting for centuries. After two years of educational trips to Trappist breweries in Europe and the construction of new facilities, Spencer's abbey became the first non-European Trappist brewery.

Its production and commercial choices are similar those of other craft breweries in the USA, making it somewhat of an outlier among Trappist-run brewing operations. In just 5 years, it has produced 10 different beers, which are divided into three product lines: "Trappist Classics," "American Trappist Craft Beers" (with a canned IPA, two Lagers, and the Imperial Stout profiled below), and finally the "Spencer Fruit Series," which includes two outstanding beers: Spencer Peach Saison and Spencer Grapefruit IPA.

Profile

Appearance: *pitch-black color, with a very thick, tan head*
Aroma: *dominated by roasted malt, mocha coffee, and chocolate, with nuances of caramel, blackberries, and umami*
Mouthfeel: *medium-full body, roasted malt, burnt caramel, slightly bitter licorice, and roots*
Overall Impression: *a fairly classic Imperial Stout, with moderate complexity and balance*

Zundert 10

Style: *BELGIAN SPECIALITY ALE (QUARUPEL)*

ABV: *10%*
Fermentation: *Top*
Bottle: *11 fl oz (0.33 l) with a crown cap*
Producer: *The Trappists of Our Lady*
of Refuge (Maria Toevlucht) abbey
in Zundert
Locality: *Zundert*
(Northern Brabant – the Netherlands)

The first Trappists to migrate to the Netherlands came from the French monastery of Mont des Cats. They settled in Tilburg, where, in 1881, they founded the Koningshoeven Abbey. The historic Trappist brewery La Trappe is also located there. In 1897, a noblewoman from Zundert donated some of her land to the abbot of Koningshoeven, who used it to build an abbey called Our Lady of Refuge that offered refuge to French monks fleeing religious persecution in France. Dairy cattle breeding and agriculture were the traditional means of financial support for Our Lady of Refuge, but after the year 2000, the collapse of milk prices and other economic challenges forced the monks to seek new ways of earning money. They decided to start a Trappist brewery called De Kievit (The Lapwing), named after a bird that was once widespread in the area. The lapwing also serves as the brewery's logo.

In 2013, Our Lady of Refuge became the ninth-largest beer-producing Trappist abbey in the world and the second-largest in the Netherlands. It currently produces only two beers, both in the style of the Old Trappists. According to tradition, each beer includes a number in its name to indicate its alcohol content: Zundert 8 (a Tripel with 8% ABV), and Zundert 10 (a Quadrupel with 10% ABV).

Profile
Appearance: *very dark amber color; compact, beige head with good persistence*
Aroma: *caramel, banana, dry and tropical fruit, licorice, cocoa, phenolic*
Mouthfeel: *creamy full body, smooth effervescence; sweet taste that includes molasses, dried figs; bitter finish*
Overall Impression: *rich and sumptuous, recommended for all lovers of the Quadrupel style*

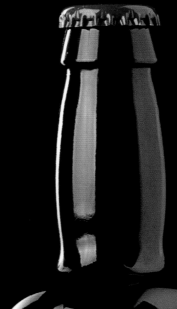

ENGLISH TRAPPIST ALE

STRONG ALE BREWED BY THE MONKS OF MOUNT
SAINT BERNARD ABBEY, CHARNWOOD FOREST

ALC. 7.4% VOL

Tynt Meadow English Trappist Ale

Style: *STRONG ALE*

ABV: *7.4%*
Fermentation: *Top*
Bottle: *11 fl oz (0.33 l) with a crown cap*

Producer: *The Trappists of Mount St. Bernard abbey*
Locality: *Coalville (Leicestershire – UK)*

The Trappist settlement of Mount St. Bernard began in 1835 at the behest of Ambrose de Lisle, an Anglican layman who converted to Catholicism. He donated land to the monks, which included a dilapidated cottage in the Tynt Meadow section of Charnwood forest. The monks established an abbey there and decided to call it Mount St. Bernard. Safe from the turmoil of the French Revolution, the monks of Tynt Meadow thrived, dedicating themselves primarily to farming, cattle breeding, and cheesemaking. However, after fluctuations in the agriculture industry and the collapse of milk prices, Mount St. Bernard, like their Dutch counterparts in Zundert, had to find new ways of earning money. The monks decided to bring back a tradition that the abbey had abandoned decades before: brewing. They began visiting microbreweries in the area, new monastic breweries in Norcia and Saint-Wandrille, and of course the historic Trappist breweries in Belgium and the Netherlands. After acquiring firsthand brewing knowledge and building the necessary facilities, the monks were soon in business. Instead of imitatating Belgian Trappist beers, they decided to focus on British styles. Currently they brew only one beer, the English Trappist Ale. Its name is meant to highlight the fact that Trappists aren't just found in Belgium!

Profile

Appearance: *dark brown color with reddish highlights; slightly hazy, with a medium, off-white head*
Aroma: *dark caramel, chestnut honey, carob, hazelnut, dried plum, ripe fruit*
Mouthfeel: *medium body, moderate effervescence; chocolatey and white peppery feel; bitter finish*
Overall Impression: *great balance between sweetness, bitterness, and alcohol without being overwhelming*

Saison and Farmhouse Ales

The origins of Saison can be traced back to farms in Wallonia, Belgium. It was brewed by hardworking farmers who wanted a thrist-quenching beer satisfying enough to serve as a meal in a bottle. Farm laborers were sometimes paid in Saison, which they could sell themselves (or, more often, drink). Farmers rarely bothered with strict recipes, instead choosing to improvise each batch depending on their own tastes and the availability of local ingredients. As the farmers of Wallonia often had to work in the hot sun all day, Saisons were designed to be light in alcohol, citrusy, slightly bitter, and a little spicy. There was just one caveat: they all had to be consumed by the end of summer, otherwise they would go sour.

Because Saison has such a loose history, its presence in the beer industry is confusing. Many wildy different beers are labeled Saisons. To make matters worse, American breweries often use the name Farmhouse Ale instead of Saison, though both generally refer to bitter, hop-forward, gold-colored beers.

To capture the essence of this chaotic style, we've included several beers as unlike each other as separate species: the Saison Dupont by Brasserie Dupont, a simple, classic Saison; the American Standard Farmhouse by Prairie-Krebs, a more contemporary choice; and lastly, La Saison $\sqrt{225}$ by Swiss brewery BFM, a complex Saison aged in oak barrels.

Saison Dupont

Style: SAISON

ABV: *6.5%*

Producer: *Brasserie Dupo...*

Fermentation: *Top*

Locality: *Tourpes*

...0.33 l) with a crown cap

(Wallonia – Belgium)

...t is housed on an old farm. It became a farm b...
...ey and Saison beers. In 1920, the property p...
...pont family, who still own it a century (and fiv...
...n Dupont recipe we are familiar with today w...
...ather Luis Dupont, an agronomist who wante...
...ewed by the farm brewery in the 1800s.
...son Dupont—considered a standard-bearer o...
...all Belgian Saisons—is actually a modern S...
...f the past. Packed with earthy, spicy, and sub...
...ds our ideas of what a Saison can do.
...ont's popularity continues to rise. If you're h...
...uld be your next choice. It's a great beer with ...
...d a bready, yeasty aroma. A taste of the Belgi...

Profile

...earance: *old gold color, slightly hazy (the yeast sed...*
make it cloudy); abundant white head that fades q...
...ic Dupont-yeast aroma; peppery, fruity, herbaceous...
...edium-light body, great effervescence, citrus fruits,...
with a fairly dry finish
...ression: *simple, fresh, thirst-quenching; the beauty...*
in its simplicity

PRAIRIE
ARTISAN ALES

How to Noodle

STANDARD
A HOPPY FARMHOUSE ALE

Standard
A Hoppy Farmhouse Ale

Style: *FARMHOUSE*

ABV: *5.6%* **Producer:** *Prairie Artisan Ales*
Fermentation: *Top* *(Krebs Brewing Company)*
Can: *11 fl oz (0.33 l)* **Locality:** *Krebs (Oklahoma – USA)*

Chase and Colin Healey, two highly experienced homebrewers, are the masterminds behind this brew. They started out in 2012 creating beer recipes and having them produced by local breweries. With the first year's proceeds, they were able to build their own brewery, and by the end of 2013, they started brewing beers on their own.

Today, they still define themselves as a "small, third-wave brewery from Oklahoma," but their business has become a craft brew poster-child of sorts, inspiring thousands of other homebrewers to try to expand their operations.

For those of you who only trust beer-rating sites, you should know that, in 2016, Prairie Artisan Ales made it onto the list of the world's top 100 breweries. It is now the top brewery in Oklahoma, and several of its beers have landed on the list of the world's top 100 beers. Prairie offers a wide range of beers, from barrel-aged dark ales to beers brewed with wine, champagne, and wild yeast. Its Standard Hoppy Farmhouse Ale is a modern Saison characterized by Motueka hops from New Zealand. If you're interested in just how complex a Saison can get, give this one a pour.

Profile
Appearance: *hazy, light-gold color, with a thick, white head that fades quickly*
Aroma: *citrusy and herbaceous, with the typical spiciness of Saison yeast*
Mouthfeel: *medium-light body, with a spicy, lime flavor*
Overall Impression: *a fresh and light everyday beer*

La Saison √225

Style: *SAISON*

ABV: *6%*
Fermentation: *Top*
Bottle: *11 fl oz (0.33 l) with a flip-top*

Producer: *Brasserie des Franches-Montagnes (BFM)*
Locality: *Saignelégier (Jura – Switzerland)*

BFM, a pioneer in the revival of brewing in Europe, was founded in 1997 in Switzerland, the homeland of its founder, Jerome Rebetez. An oenologist and one of the very first modern homebrewers, Rebetez built his brewery with the prize money he won in a televised brewing competition.

The originality of this brewery's beers, which stood out right from the start, perfectly reflect Rebetez's quirky personality. The square root of 225 is 15, a clever tribute to BFM's 15th anniversary, which it celebrated in 2012. This beer is Jerome's nod to Saisons of the past, as well as a protest against many current Saison beers on the market, which contain all sorts of ingredients that have nothing to do with the history of the farmers in Wallonia. He describes this beer as "the reconstruction of a centuries-old sour beer." The brew is aged in third-use Abbay de Saint bon Chien barrels for 4 months, which is where its signature sourness comes from.

Profile

Appearance: *deep, golden color, almost orange; liquid is transparent, but with sediment at the bottom of the bottle*

Aroma: *very funky aroma offering racy citrus fruit with a fruity background (from white grapes to pineapple), plus a hint of acetic acid*

Mouthfeel: *light body, high carbonation, lactic acidity, with loads of fruit and a bitter finish*

Overall Impression: *an old-style Saison enjoyable long after summer is over; an extremely thirst-quenching Sour Saison*

Smoked Beers

This group includes any beer characterized by smoky aromas and flavors. All classic beer styles can be smoked, as long as the smoke doesn't destroy or obstruct the style's typical flavors. Smoke must be a balanced addition, and it must pair well with the base of the beer and enrich it without overwhelming its profile. Today you can find many special-edition smoked beers on the market that aren't based on any particular style. These brews often include extra ingredients such as fruit and spices.

Smoked beers aren't generally created through any particular production process. Instead, they are made with pre-smoked ingredients, the most common being barley malt. The barley malt is smoked during malting, usually during the drying stage when, in addition to being subjected to heat, the wet and swollen grains have smoke filtered through them, which they absorb. The smoke is produced by burning hard aromatic woods (such as beech, oak, maple, or cherry), or peat, although peat is more common in the production of peated whiskeys.

Keep in mind that, prior to the 19th century, most barley malt was dried over wood fires. Therefore almost all beers on the market at that time would have had a smoky tinge to them.

Aecht Sclenkerla Rauchbier

Style: *MARZEN RAUCHBIER*

ABV: *5.1%*
Fermentation: *Bottom*
Bottle: *17 fl oz (0.5 l) with a crown cap*

Producer: *Heller-Brau Trum*
Locality: *Bamberg*
(Franconia-Bavaria – Germany)

Bamberg is the world capital of *Rauchbiers* (smoked beers), and Schlenkerla is the queen of them all. If you get the chance one day, try sampling this excellent beer in the old Schlenkerla tavern, which is right next to Schlenkerla's brewery, and you'll understand what all the fuss is about. The tavern is in the heart of Bamberg's old town, at number 6 Dominikanerstraße to be exact. It is housed in a former Dominican convent, and it serves the original Schlenkerla smoked beer on tap, from oak barrels. If you're fortunate enough to get one of the 10 tables inside the Dominikanerklause room (an ancient chapel dating back to 1300), the experience would be complete.

According to legend, the beer's secret lies in the unique type of beech wood used to smoke it, which is seasoned for 3 years, but the truth is that Schlenkerla is one of the few breweries that doesn't buy its smoked malts from outside vendors. Instead, they prepare it on-site, in the brewery's malt house. The name Schlenkerla roughly translates to "person with a limp," and is attributed to the awkward gait of Andreas Graser, Schlenkerla's owner and brewer who, in 1877, supposedly injured his leg while transporting a barrel of beer. Schlenkerla's tavern and brewery are run by Graser's heirs to this day.

Profile

Appearance: *brown color with ruby highlights; clear, with a wispy and fairly persistent creamy, beige head*
Aroma: *intense smoky notes, reminiscent of speck ham and smoked scamorza cheese, with hints of caramel and rye bread*
Mouthfeel: *the smoky flavor is supported by loads of caramel malt and a nice body*
Overall Impression: *strong, intense, but incredibly clean in the finish; a perfect example of the smoked style*

BIRRA DEL CARROBIOLO

PICCOLO OPIFICIO BRASSICOLO CARROBIOLO

11.11
O.G.

X-TRA PEATED

2018 SPECIAL EDITION

ALC 13% VOL. | BIRRA STAGIONALE INVERNALE | 75 I.B.U.

RIFERMENTATA

O.G. 1111
Winter Warmer

Style: *EXTRA STRONG PEATED OLD ALE*

ABV: *13%*
Fermentation: *Top*
Bottle: *12.7 fl oz (0.375 l) with a crown cap*

Producer: *Piccolo Opificio Brassicolo del Carrobiolo FERMENTUM*
Locality: *Monza (Lombardy – Italy)*

This small brewery was established in 2008 inside a former convent in the center of Monza, Italy. Contrary to current microbrewery trends, the brewery has chosen to evolve into a brewpub rather than ramp up its production capacities. According to Pietro Fontana (aka yours truly), the goal has always been to embody the spirit of an independent, regional microbrewery, which allows brewers maximum freedom to produce creative brews. As much beer as possible is served on-site, pumped directly from maturation tanks, as this removes the hassle of bottling and shipping. Most importantly, this setup cuts out all intermediaries, creating an intimate drinking experience in which customers are served personally by the people actually responsible for brewing the beer.

O.G. 1111 is inspired by traditional ales, though this version is extra strong. It's intended as a winter warmer (hence the flames on the label), so drinking it should help keep you nice and toasty on cold days. Its high alcohol content packs additional heat, though this creeps up slowly, like a devil's pitchfork rising out of the flames. O.G. 1111 has also been designed to capture the powerful dryness and aromaticity of peated whiskeys, evoking the taste of peat smoked over burning embers.

Profile

Appearance: *light mahogany with orange hues; clear, with an off-white head that fades quickly*

Aroma: *marine peat, iodine, mooring rope, dates, prunes, spirit-soaked black cherries, and raisins*

Mouthfeel: *medium-light body, caramel, with a bitter aftertaste of quinine and rhubarb*

Overall Impression: *a winter warmer meant as a nod to the great peated whiskeys, though with a sugary swirl of bitters*

Imperial Stout

Along with IPAs and Sours, Imperial Stouts are probably the most popular beer style at the moment. Some breweries add the word "Russian" to the name, as that was the way Stouts were often marketed in 18th-century England, but "Imperial Stout" usually refers to a dark, rich, high-alcohol beer. Imperial Stouts were indeed born in England, along with Porters and other styles of Stout. Darker beers were hugely popular throughout the Victorian era. After WWII, Imperial Stouts declined, and by the 1980s, they had almost entirely disappeared. Theories abound as to why this happened, but in general it's believed that Imperial Stout recipes were simply too expensive for industrial producers to make. The beer's strong taste may have also been too overpowering for many beer consumers. These days, much to our delight, craft microbreweries have put Imperial Stout back on the map. We can only imagine how happy philosopher Giambattista Vico would be knowing that his theory of "historic recurrence" has been proven correct.

There are now endless interpretations of the Imperial Stout on the market. Some are barrel-aged, some are made with Brettanomyces or other wild yeasts, and some contain creative ingredients like coffee, cocoa, rye, oats, or mushrooms! Imperial Stouts are often released as one-off beers meant to be snapped up by beer geeks willing to pay high prices for them, but they've also become permanent fixtures in the beer world.

Rasputin

Style: *IMPERIAL STOUT*

ABV: *10.4%*   **Producer:** *Brouwerij De Molen*
Fermentation: *Top*   **Locality:** *Bodegraven*
Bottle: *11 fl oz (0.33 l) with a crown cap*   *(South Holland – the Netherlands)*

In 2004, De Molen brewery began its brewing adventures in a picturesque, though rather cramped, former mill (hence the name and logo). The beers it started brewing garnered public attention immediately, though craft beer enthusiasts also took note, falling in love with their strong beers and simple, hand-drawn labels. The labels also provide detailed information about each beer's ingredients—a marketing tactic that has since spread industry-wide. De Molen became known for its fearless experimentation thanks to its speed in releasing new products, its one-off beers, and its collaborations with other breweries. Menno Olivier (De Molen's founder) is now a homebrew legend, with many homebrewers dreaming of replicating his sucess. De Molen opened a new headquarters in 2011 to maximize its output, though this may have dented their microbrew reputation. In 2016, BAVARIA Industries Group AG (the Netherlands' second-largest beer producer after Heineken) acquired a 35% share of De Molen. In 2018, BAVARIA Industries Group changed its name to Swinkels Family Brewers in a bid to seem more authentic. Shortly after that, Swinkels bought De Molen outright, shocking legions of beer aficionados. It remains to be seen whether De Molen will be able to produce beer of the same high quality now that its management has changed so drastically. In any case, Menno Olivier continues to inspire homebrewers everywhere who hope to one day sell their businesses to larger entities.

Profile

Appearance: *dark brown color, with a small, fairly persistent sand-colored head*
Aroma: *coffee and dark chocolate, dark red fruit, molasses, and soy sauce*
Mouthfeel: *medium-full body, roasted malt, licorice, caramel, prune, and tobacco*
Overall Impression: *averagely complex and balanced, with a slight acidity in the finish*

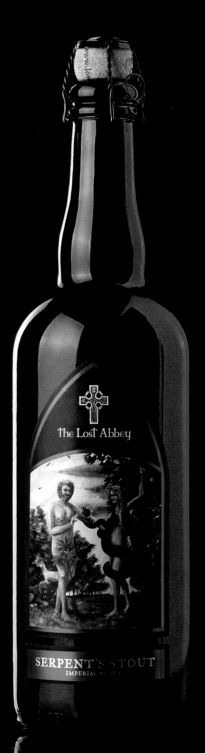

Serpent's Stout
Vintage 2019

Style: *IMPERIAL STOUT*

ABV: *11%* **Producer:** *The Lost Abbey*
Fermentation: *Top* **Locality:** *San Marcos*
Bottle: *25 fl oz (0.75 l) with a mushroom cork* *(California – USA)*

The Lost Abbey and Port Brewing are both brands of Port Brewing Company. They share a facility in San Marcos, California that used to house Stone Brewing Company. Although similar in quality, they are two distinct brands with two distinct beer lines. The breweries officially opened their doors in 2006 and immediately started winning cascades of awards and prizes. The enterprise is actually a spin-off of Pizza Port, a California brewpub managed by master brewer Tomme Arthur. The Lost Abbey brand pays homage to the monastic brewing traditions of Belgium, but it also specializes in barrel-aged beers and sours. We could have featured The Lost Abbey's award-winning brown ale Cuvee de Tomme, but that would have been predictable. Plus, that one happens to be a creation of Pizza Port's, not The Lost Abbey or Port Brewing. Instead, we chose to go with Serpent's Stout, an annual winter release and one of The Lost Abbey's few non-Belgian-inspired beers.

This beer is so thick and rich that it seeps out of the bottle very slowly. It has a powerful aroma and mouthfeel, flexing all its muscles and showing off its 11% alcohol content. After the first sip, it transforms into a gentle, sophisticated beer. This one isn't for everyone, but neither is it hard to love.

Profile

Appearance: *black color, with a thin, cappuccino-like head that fades quickly*
Aroma: *roasted coffee beans, licorice, plum jam, figs, and dates; Madeira wine; leathery, ethery*
Mouthfeel: *full-bodied and oily; coffee, roasted barley, dark chocolate, vanilla*
Overall Impression: *an extremely long and powerful aftertaste that enhances its complexity*

Sticky Wings

Style: *DOUBLE MASH IMPERIAL RYE STOUT*

ABV: *9%* **Producer:** *Dok Brewing Company*
Fermentation: *Top* **Locality:** *Gent*
Bottle: *17 fl oz (0.5 l) with a crown cap* *(East Flanders – Belgium)*

Dok Brewing Company is a recent brewpub housed in an old warehouse in the Dok-Noord area of Gent, Belgium. Established in May of 2018, it's equipped with a simple, on-site brewery built in a post-industrial style. It's inspired more by the craft beer revolution than it is by classic Belgium beer culture. Its young brewers, beer sommeliers, and homebrewers have traveled the world and discovered which tastes suit them. They didn't want to limit themselves to just one style, so their operation is constantly in flux. Don't expect to always find the same products. When one beer ends, another one begins, and it will most likely be much different than its predecessor. The Sticky Wings featured here—a double mash Imperial Stout produced with a large percentage of rye—is bottled, but not all their products are.

The on-site brewery is mounted on steel frames and has a 265-gallon (10 hl) brewing tank, 530-gallon (20 hl) fermenters, two maturation tanks, and two serving tanks. Beer is pumped directly from the latter at an adjoining counter. The brewpub boasts 30 beers on tap. Some are homebrewed, but many are guest beers from all over the world.

Profile

Appearance: *pitch-black color, with a moderately persistent, beige head*
Aroma: *roasted malt, chocolate, dark malts, spices, fruit (blueberry, cherry, plum), molasses, licorice*
Mouthfeel: *rich, sweet, malty, spicy; rye bread; notes of chocolate, licorice, molasses; sneaks in a touch of honey*
Overall Impression: *very smooth, with a little bitterness to balance it out; a great dessert beer*

Odravein Bourbon
Bourbon Barrel Aged
Barley Wine

Our anniversary
barley wine, aged in
bourbon barrels.

Põhjala pruulikoja
aastapäevaks
pruulitud barley
wine, mis on
laagerdunud
bourbon-viski
vaatides.

Barrel-Aged

Until the early 20th century, the fermentation, maturation, and transportation of beer happened inside wooden barrels. Eventually these were abandoned in favor of metal (fermenters, kegs, cans) and glass (bottles). We usually associate barrels with wine, whiskey, and rum. Today, most beer styles don't require barrels, but their ability to add complex characteristics, including vanilla, tannins, roasted malt, and oxidation, is another new front being explored by craft breweries.

You could potentially age any type of beer in barrels, but it's generally preferable to use structured beers with higher alcohol contents or styles that require roasted malts. Beers with these properties have fuller bodies that are better able to withstand oxidation and the introduction of tannins and richer flavors. All Imperial Stouts—Barley Wine, Porter, Brown Ale, and Strong Belgian Ale (both pale and dark)—can benefit from time in barrels. In many cases, the barrels used to age beer have already held other alcoholic beverages first. Whiskey, bourbon, rum, and wine barrels are popular choices, as these drinks have strong characteristics that will permeate the beer and increase its complexity.

Oak is the standard wood used for most barrels. The size of the barrel is also important: the smaller the barrel, the less beer it can hold and thus the more flavor it will ultimately impart. Barrel fermentation and barrel-aging are still being rediscovered, but so far the results have been exciting.

Oerbier
Special Reserva 2015

Style: *BELGIAN STRONG DARK ALE - BARREL-AGED*

ABV: *13%*
Fermentation: *Top*
Bottle: *25 fl oz (0.75 l)*

with a cork stopper + crown cap
Producer: *De Dolle Brouwers*
Locality: *Esen (Belgium)*

In 1980, the De Dolle brothers took over a historic brewing building in West Flanders, Belgium and began producing their own brews. Their products are a constant source of reassurance for fans of complex Belgian beers. Oerbier was De Dolle's first creation, a Belgian Strong Ale which, like the brewery, has evolved over time. In 2000, for example, when the strain of yeast that characterized it was discontinued, the De Dolle brothers created a new yeast and allowed production to continue. It took them several attempts, but eventually they landed on the perfect replacement, and today the yeast they created is coveted by brewers all over the world. Oerbier's high alcohol content and complex structure make it perfect for barrel-aging, and that's exactly what the De Dolle brothers did when creating the Oerbier Reserva. For the 2015 version, they used Bordeaux wine casks.

Another of the brewery's goodies is Stille Nacht (Silent Night), which is released around the Christmas season every year. Beer fans eagerly await its arrival, hoping to be among the first to taste it on tap. Bottles of it can be bought and aged at home. Home-aging with Stille Nacht is an experiment. Unlike Oerbier, Stille Nacht will sometimes dry out when aged in the bottle.

Profile

Appearance: *dark copper-brown, hazy, with an ivory head that fades quickly*
Aroma: *winey, balsamic; red fruits with hints of chocolate, spices, and nutmeg*
Mouthfeel: *acidity from the red fruit; balsamic vinegar, woody notes, smooth toffee, with a warm and slightly smoky finish*
Overall Impression: *complex and balanced notes of wood and wine imparted by the barrel; a softness attributable to the lactic acid*

Odravein Bourbon BA

Style: *BARLEY WINE, BARREL-AGED*

ABV: *14%*
Fermentation: *Top*
Bottle: *11 fl oz (0.33 l) crown cap + wax seal*

Producer: *Põhjala*
Locality: *Tallinn*
(Estonia)

Põhjala (an Estonian brewery) is an excellent example of the wave of innovative breweries that have opened since 2010. In just a few years, they've created a consistent and thriving niche, starting with the relatively small Estonian market and slowly conquering the rest of the world. Their products range from basic styles to a huge selection of Imperial Stouts reimagined in provocative ways. Põhjala also enjoys collaborating with breweries in other countries.

Odravein Bourbon BA is a Barley Wine aged in bourbon barrels. It was produced for the brewery's anniversary and is part of its Cellar Series project, which includes several well-rated beers aged in different types of barrels (bourbon, cognac, sherry, tequila, and many others). Overall, it's an elegant beer that skillfully blends the flavor of bourbon with the lively and fruity tastes typical of Barley Wine.

Profile

Appearance: *mahogany brown color with ruby red highlights and a white head that fades quickly*

Aroma: *caramel, raspberry jam, vanilla, and lemon curd, which become more evident over time*

Mouthfeel: *vanilla in the foreground; sensations of almost all the aromas, with evident spicy notes (ginger); a long finish in which the alcohol is present; a blending of caramel and a faint metallic taste*

Overall Impression: *the typical structure of Barley Wine balances the woody and vanilla notes from the barrels without overpowering it; a complex beer not everyone will appreciate*

Telemachus

Style: *AMERICAN WILD ALE – BARREL-AGED SOUR DARK ALE*

ABV: *7.5%*
Fermentation: *Spontaneous*
Bottle: *25 fl oz (0.75 l) with a cork stopper*

Producer: *Pen Druid Brewing*
Locality: *Rappahannock*
(Virginia – USA)

Pen Druid Brewing is an all-American brewery. It was founded in Virginia in 2015 by three brothers: Lain, Van, and Jennings Carney. The name Pen Druid comes from their old family farm, which is located a few miles downstream from the brewery. Their project is an ambitious one: they only use barrels for fermentation and maturation. On top of that, they only ferment their beers with their own wild yeasts foraged from around Rappahannock County. They carbonate naturally, using secondary fermentations in bottles and kegs. All this wasn't complicated enough, so they decided they had to only use wood-fired kettles. The result is a selection of extremely unique, limited-production American Wild Ale-style beers. Telemachus is a Sour Dark Ale that incorporates as many local ingredients as possible, from well water to wild yeasts and hops. It's fermented and aged in barrels for 15 months. This one tastes almost like an American Oud Bruin (Old Brown) and could easily be mistaken for a Sour. These guys are eclectic, to say the least. Brave, innovative, and forward-thinking, each of their beers is an experience.

Profile
Appearance: *slightly hazy brown color, with an abundant beige head that fades quickly*
Aroma: *dried fruit, raisins; notes of balsamic and caramel that emerge slowly*
Mouthfeel: *the initial slight acidity gives way to notes of raspberry, blackberry, raisin, and a touch of caramel; light body with evident carbonation*
Overall Impression: *good carbonation and body; the acidity is never too high; despite the 7.5% alcohol, this one is surprisingly easy to drink*

Lambic

Lambics are generally referred to as "spontaneously fermented sour beers," but not all spontaneously fermented sour beers can be called Lambics! In fact, the term "Lambic" is protected by both Belgium and the European Union and can only be applied to traditional beers made in the Pajottenland region of Belgium. Spontaneous fermentation is achieved by leaving the wort to cool in large, open-air vats. The inoculation (the moment when yeast and bacteria come into contact with liquid) is left up to whatever organisms happen to be in the air or on the fruit that's being fermented. The results are highly unique—a description that can also be applied to Lambic beers. Lambics are produced with aged hops. With aged hops, the beer still gets antimicrobial properties that reduce the amount of bacteria and allow wild yeast to take hold early in the aging process. Lambic flavors can be difficult for newbies to appreciate. At the end of the brewing process, you can serve a Lambic straight from the barrel. However, Lambics can also be blended to make Oude Gueuze (a blend of young and old Lambics that undergoes secondary fermentation in the bottle without any added sugar), or the more generic Gueuze (the same as Oude Gueuze but with sugar added). There are also fruit Lambics, which have fruit added to them (cherries and raspberries are popular choices) during the maturation process. The yeasts and bacteria then ferment all the sugars present in the added fruit. Lambics are brewed only in the fall and winter and are a primary example of just how complicated beer-making can get!

Geuze Mariage Parfait

Style: *OUDE GUEUZE*

ABV: *8%*
Fermentation: *Spontaneous*
Bottle: *12.7 fl oz (0.375 l) with a cork stopper*

Producer: *Brouwerij Boon*
Locality: *Lembeek (Belgium)*

In the mid-1970s, Frank Boon took over a historic brewery in Lembeek, Belgium, that had been in operation since 1680. Since the late 19th-century, it had been producing Lambics. The 1970s were a bad time for Lambics. Larger beer conglomerates had successfully consolidated the beer industry. Frank Boon renamed the brewery after himself and revitalized the Gueuze style, creating an iconic brand that is now recognized all over the world. At the same time, Boon remains a brewery more focused on brewing prowess than market dominance. It has a great line of products, such as Mariage Parfait, which is an excellent value for the money. Its Oude Geuzes are sold at competitive prices in 8.5 fl oz (250 ml) bottles. Mariage Parfait is a classic Oude Gueuze (meaning it has no added sugar) and a vintage beer with a high alcohol content. Its vintage is determined by the year of the oldest Lambic in the blend. Mariage Parfait is indeed a perfect marriage between 95% mild Lambic—aged at least three years and specially selected by Frank—and 5% young Lambic. After natural secondary fermentation in the bottle and a few months of resting, the beer is put on the market with a twenty-year expiration date. The result is a complex, well-balanced, and multifaceted beer that produces a warming mouthfeel. One of the best examples of this style available.

Profile

Appearance: *hazy, golden color with amber highlights; a white head that fades quickly*
Aroma: *citric acid, lemon peel, green apple with a peachy streak, vanilla, and hints of leather and cellars*
Mouthfeel: *acidic hints of ripe fruit and vanilla; an almost woody sensation*
Overall Impression: *a very complex beer with a surprising smoothness; leaves the mouth feeling clean and fresh*

Brett-Elle

Style: *OUDE GUEUZE*

ABV: *5.5%*

Fermentation: *Spontaneous*

Bottle: *12.7 fl oz (0.375 l) with a cork stopper + crown cap*

Producer: *Lambiek Fabriek*

Locality: *Sint-Pieters-Leeuw (Belgium)*

Lambiek Fabriek is still extremely new. It was started in 2016 by three friends—Jo Van Aert, Jo Panneels, and Jozef Van Bosstraeten—all of whom are passionate about Lambics. They started experimenting with home blends in 2000, purchasing ingredients from various producers. When ingredients became too expensive and demand for their brews started increasing, they were forced to consider going professional. Jo Van Aert, a brewer at Belgoo, agreed to let Lambiek Fabriek brew Lambics on-site at Belgoo. Brett-Elle, a new-generation Oude Gueuze, was Lambiek Fabriek's first product. The first blends were made with a young Lambic, aged 1–2 years, and a Lambic aged for at least 4 years. The older Lambic had to come from another brewery due to the aging required. Lambiek Fabriek's barrels are still housed in Belgoo. Since the operation is still quite new, the production of this beer will undoubtedly continue to evolve over time. Brett-Elle is a pleasant, fruity Gueuze with just the right amount of acidity.

Lambiek Fabriek is now a member of HORAL, the High Council for Artisanal Lambic Beers (*Hoge Raad voor Ambachtelijke Lambiekbieren*, in Dutch), a consortium of Lambic brewers and blenders that protects and promotes traditional Lambic beer culture.

Profile

Appearance: *golden yellow color, slightly hazy, with a quick-fading white head*

Aroma: *delicate, woody, and simple; green apple, citric acid, dried apricot*

Mouthfeel: *slightly sour, pungent, lemon peel, hints of Brettanomyces*

Overall Impression: *easy to drink, refreshing, and not at all sharp, with aromas and flavors that never overpower*

vée des Jacobi

Red Sour Ale with pronounc
cascade of beautiful, comp
fermentation imbues Rong
od, apple and cherries. Oak
18 months imparts a gentle
Full-bodied and delicious

FLEMISH
SOUR ALE

Product of Belgium

Barrel J Aged

BIERE DE
FOUDRE

uvée

Other Sours

In addition to Lambics, there are many other Sours, traditional and otherwise, that deserve our attention, including Berliner Weisses, Flanders Red Ales (featured in the pages that follow), Oud Bruins, Goses, and American Wild Ales. Bacteria gives Sours their unique taste, while the yeast adds bready, earthy qualities. Sours have exploded in popularity in recent years.

Oud Bruins, typical of East Flanders, Belgium, are mixed-fermentation (yeast + lactobacillus + acetobacter) sweet-and-sour beers matured in steel tanks. They are less acidic and alcoholic compared to Flanders Red Ales. Their brownish color comes from the dark malts used to brew them. Oud Bruin is a classic beer style that dates back to at least the 17th century.

Goses are traditional German beers. They originated in the German city of Goslar, on the Gose river. The height of their success was at the end of the 19th century, in Leipzig, where there were roughly 80 *Gosenschenkes* ("Gose taverns"). By the end of World War II, they were no longer produced in East Germany. Traditionally, Gose beers were spontaneously fermented and brewed with river water, which is quite salty. Today the salt is added, and its moderate acidity comes from mixed fermentation and the addition of lactic bacteria. Goses are produced with large quantities of wheat and flavored with coriander seeds.

American Wild Ales represent a generic group of beers characterized by various microorganisms and wild yeasts. This category is a catchall for a wide range of "wild" beers that don't conform to traditional, European Sour standards.

Crianza III

Style: *FLANDERS RED ALE*

ABV: *7.4%*
Fermentation: *Top + mixed*
Bottle: *11 fl oz (0.33 l) with a crown cap*

Producer: *Brasserie de la Senne*
Locality: *Brussels (Belgium)*

Flanders Red Ales are brewed in West Flanders, Belgium. They are complex Sours dominated by acetic acid and woody, vinous notes acquired through time spent in barrels. They usually mature in large oak barrels for 1–2 years. Strains of Saccharomyces (often wild) are used during fermentation, along with Brettanomyces, Lactobacillus, and Acetobacter.

Bernard Leboucq and Yvan de Baets started brewing in 2003, but it was only a few years and several locations later, in 2010, that they finally managed to open their own brewery in Brussels. They decided to call it Brasserie de la Senne in honor of the famous La Senne river that flows nearby.

Crianza III is a mixed-fermentation Flanders Red Ale aged for just over a year in oak barrels. It's a little tamer than other, more traditional Flanders Red Ales, so it should really be thought of as a modern reinterpretation. Its mineral and slightly sour tastes make it wonderfully refreshing.

Profile

Appearance: *hazy, dark-amber color with bright highlights; a fairly persistent white head*

Aroma: *citric acid, green apple, red fruit; a touch of caramel and plum*

Mouthfeel: *the citric acid is subdued; red fruit, a little spicy; well-balanced by the pleasant sweetness of ripe fruit and caramel; a dry and slightly tannic finish*

Overall Impression: *very refined for a Flanders Red Ale; the acetic acid and vinous notes are almost nonexistent; a few funky notes emerge shyly if the beer is given time to warm up and oxygenate in the glass*

TRUE AUTHENTIC
BERLINER WEISSE

STONE

WHITE GHOST

Berliner

WEISSE

Cl.331   BERLIN · GERMANY   Ac.4.7%

White Ghost

Style: *BERLINER WEISSE*

ABV: *4.7%* **Producer:** *Stone Brewing Company*
Fermentation: *Top* **Locality:** *Berlin (Germany)/Escondido*
Can: *11 fl oz (0.33 l)* *(California – USA)*

Berliner Weisse was on the verge of extinction before homebrewers and craft brewers came to the rescue. They tend to be very drinkable, low-alcohol beers made with 2–5 pounds of wheat for every pound of barley. Their sourness comes from the lactic-acid-producing bacteria added during fermentation. In general, they are light on the hop flavor. Traditionally they were served with raspberry syrup or herbal-green woodruff to balance the acidity. Many brewers now choose to add in different fruits during fermentation.

Stone Brewing Company, a California-based brewery, was founded in 1996. Over the years, it has become one of the largest craft breweries in the United States. In 2016, it opened a satellite brewery in Berlin, Germany, that also boasted a large restaurant and beer garden. With a foothold in Germany, Stone Brewing hoped to conquer the rest of Europe. But sadly the experiment ended in 2019, when Stone sold its Berlin brewery to Scotland's BrewDog. It may be that, when it comes to craft beer, consumers are beginning to favor regionality over brand recognition.

White Ghost is a modern reinterpretation of a traditional Berliner Weisse. It has a sharp, lean lactic-acid flavor and a higher alcohol content. Stone offers this one in a can instead of a bottle—another modern touch.

Profile

Appearance: *hazy, straw-yellow color, with an abundant white head that fades quickly*
Aroma: *apricot and yellow fruit, lemon, with a background of tropical fruit and green apples*
Mouthfeel: *thin body, very effervescent; lemon, green apple, apricot, and white grapes; slightly pungent acidity*
Overall Impression: *the freshness of the beer clashes a little with the alcohol, which is slightly above average for this style*

Cuvée des Jacobins

Rouge

BIER BEER BIERE

Cuvée des Jacobins Rouge

Style: *FLEMISH SOUR ALE – BIER DE FOUDRE*

ABV: *5.5%*
Fermentation: *Spontaneous*
Bottle: *11 fl oz (0.33 l) with a crown cap*

Producer: *Brouwerij Omer Vander Ghinste*
Locality: *Bellegem (Belgium)*

The Omer Vander Ghinste Brewery is in West Flanders, Belgium, and has been in operation (and family-run, for five generations) since the end of the 19th century. From 1976 to 2014, it used the name Brasserie Bockor, taken from the name of its successful flagship beer, Bockor Pils (a Lager). It only recently went back to its historical name.

It's easy to mistake Cuvée des Jacobins Rouge for a Lambic, as it's a spontaneously fermented beer aged in French oak barrels. However, it's not brewed in the Lambic-producing region of Belgium, and it spends less time in barrels (18 months) than Lambics, which tend to age for about three years. The label of this one states that it's a Flemish Sour Ale and a "100% foederbier" (a *foeder*, or *foudre* in French, is a big barrel). The *"Rouge"* at the end of the name of course means *red*, based on its color.

The brew takes its name from Rue des Jacobins in Paris, home to Couvent Saint-Jacques, a Dominican monastery. Omer Rémi Vander Ghinste (the first Omer) lived there for a short time during WWI and decided to use the name for one of his beers.

Profile
Appearance: *slightly hazy brown color with ruby-red highlights; its beige head fades quickly*
Aroma: *cherries, caramel, dried fruit, and leather, with vinous woody notes*
Mouthfeel: *citric and acetic acid, sweet; caramel, cherry, leather, and wood, with hints of wine*
Overall Impression: *acetic acid typical of the style, never aggressive; nicely balanced by the sweetness of the caramel*

Fruit in Beer

Humans have been adding fruit to beer for centuries. Typically this was meant to enrich the flavor of the given beer while also making it more substantial. For many Lambics, the addition of fruit is part of the traditional recipe, but homebrewers and craft breweries have recently begun mixing fruit into many different styles of beer in the spirit of experimentation.

BJCP (Beer Judge Certification Program) guidelines state that fruit should complement the original style of the beer but not overwhelm it. Fruit can be added to beer in many different forms, and the chosen form will ultimately determine the robustness of the flavor. Canned and puréed fruits are popular choices, as they come pre-sanitized. Fruit can also be added together with spices. The BJCP categorizes these beers under a general Fruit and Spice Beer style. Just like with fruit, the added spice shouldn't overwhelm the profile of the beer. After all, we want to be able to taste the original flavors of the beer, not bury them under piles of fruit or spice.

If other ingredients, such as honey or molasses, are added in with the fruit, the beer is sometimes categorized under Specialty Fruit Beer. This genre of beer is growing rapidly, and even BJCP is struggling to keep up with all the new Specialty Fruit Beer products being released each year.

The use of fruit in Sours (from Berliner Weisses to American Wild Ales) and barrel-aged beers has exploded. Fruit is also sometimes added to IPAs to enhance the aromatic profile of the hops. The trend is likely to continue. Fruit gives brewers yet another tool to achieve the exact flavors they want.

Ferme de Chien

Style: FARMHOUSE ALE + CHERRIES

ABV: *5.3%*
Fermentation: *Top + brett*
Bottle: *11.8 fl oz (0.35 l) with a crown cap*

Producer: *Wicked Weed Brewing*
Locality: *Asheville*
(North Carolina – USA)

Wicked Weed Brewing opened its doors in Asheville in 2012. Its goal is to produce very hoppy American West Coast-style beers and Belgian-style, barrel-aged (and fermented) beers. In 2013, the brewery opened a second location in Candler, North Carolina, and greatly expanded its production capacities. It now hopes to become the premiere US producer of barrel-aged Sours. But Wicked Weed decided it couldn't pull off such a huge expansion alone. Five years after it began, it was sold to beer giant Ab InBev, which owns numerous high-profile brands, such as Budweiser, Corona, and Stella Artois. Another heavy loss for the world of craft brewing.

Ferme de Chien is a lightly hoppy Saison/Farmhouse Ale fermented with Brettanomyces yeast and aged in oak barrels. It is also fermented with over a pound per gallon of fresh Balaton cherries, which are a sour, dark-colored cherry native to Hungary. The name Ferme de Chien is a nod to Belgium, but the brew isn't actually related to Kriek Lambics, which also use cherries.

Profile

Appearance: *beautiful, intense ruby-red color; clear, with a thin, pinkish head that fades quickly*

Aroma: *cherries, blackberries, mixed berries; pungent, slightly floral, and spicy*

Mouthfeel: *pleasant acidity; cherries, blackberries, wood, and leather, with a bursting finish*

Overall Impression: *an elegant appearance and aroma; fresh in the mouth, though it lacks the rusticity of a Farmhouse Ale*

2015 Autumnal
Dichotomous

Style: *FRUIT AND SPICE BEER (FARMHOUSE ALE + SATSUMA)*

ABV: *6.8%*   **Producer:** *Jester King Brewery*
Fermentation: *Wild*   **Locality:** *Austin*
Bottle: *25 fl oz (0.75 l) with a crown cap*   *(Texas – USA)*

Texas-based Jester King describes itself as a "farmhouse brewery." It got its start making Farmhouse Ales with Saison yeasts before moving on to brewing mixed and spontaneously fermented beers with local ingredients. The brewery is housed on a 165-acre ranch that also includes a farm and an event hall. Jester King is also famous for having successfully sued the Texas Alcoholic Beverage Commission in a bid to change restrictive and outdated beer-labeling laws. What Jester King says regarding its brewing philosophy leaves no room for misunderstanding: "We brew what we like, drink what we want, and offer the rest to those who share our tastes."

Jester King's 2015 Autumnal Dichotomous is the seventh beer in the Dichotomous series. It's a Farmhouse Ale recirculated through cinnamon sticks and Texas satsuma zest and juice before it undergoes another two-week fermentation. Autumnal Dichotomous is produced in the fall, as the name suggests. Local seasonal ingredients are thrown in for good measure.

Because it's naturally refermented, it's best to drink this one in the fall, shortly after it's been released.

Profile

Appearance: *hazy, golden-yellow color with orange highlights; a not very persistent, abundant white head with orange streaks*
Aroma: *citric acid, mandarin, ripe fruit (pear and banana), lots of cinnamon*
Mouthfeel: *consistent aroma and minerality; sour-green apple, very dry finish; the cinnamon and spices are lost a bit in the complex flavors*
Overall Impression: *the mix of flavors is interesting, but all the clashing makes it hard to describe this one as elegant; best drunk fresh so that its spiciness can shine*

Bizarre Love Triangle

Style: *(NORDIC) SOUR + FRUIT (MANGO, PASSION FRUIT, PEACH)*

ABV: *7%*   **Producer:** *Coolhead Brew*
Fermentation: *Top*   **Locality:** *Tuusula*
Can: *11 fl oz (0.33 l)*   *(Finland)*

Coolhead Brew is a brand-new Finnish craft brewery. It opened in Tuusula in 2016 and specializes in sour beers or, as Coolhead likes to call them, Nordic Sours. Their distinctly Nordic approach to Sours involves brewing fresh, clean-tasting beers that possess hidden complexities. They also enjoy collaborating with other forward-thinking breweries.

Bizarre Love Triangle is the result of a collaboration with Fuerst Wiacek (a Berlin-based German brewery). It's a Sour (or rather, a Nordic sour!) brewed with fruit salad—err, forgive us—we mean brewed with a mix of passion fruit, mango, and peach, plus a dash of Himalayan pink salt.

Profile

Appearance: *deep-yellow color, cloudy, with a very thin white head*
Aroma: *dominantly peachy, with a background of passion fruit and mango; its herbaceous notes emerge gradually*
Mouthfeel: *the very delicate sourness is overwhelmed by peach, mango, and a long pineapple aftertaste; the herbaceous notes are fairly muted*
Overall Impression: *despite its high alcohol content, this one's an easy-to-drink beer that leaves a pleasant feeling of freshness and fruitiness in the mouth; minimalist despite its complex mix of ingredients*

India Pale Ale

The storied roots of India Pale Ale—aka IPA—lie in its heavy hopping. Soldiers and personnel of the British Empire in the east needed beer, but it was believed that India was too hot and humid for real brewing. The journey (by boat) from Britain to India took roughly six months, so the beer needed to stay fresh for that long. A brewer named George Hodgson found a solution. His Bow Brewery in London began making a heavily hopped beer that had to be aged upon arrival first before consumption. The beer's strong flavors caught on, and Hodgson soon became famous for producing and exporting IPA. It also helped that his Bow Brewery was strategically positioned near the docks of the River Thames. Eventually larger breweries (such as Bass) began making their own IPAs. The development of refrigeration meant that longer-lasting beers weren't a necessity anymore. It wasn't until the 1970s that IPAs began to reappear, although this didn't happen in Britain. American homebrewers made a hobby of recreating forgotten English beers. The IPA soon became a favorite. Today, many homebrewers and craft breweries have released their own spins on the beloved IPA. IPAs are appreciated for their bitterness and powerful hoppy aromas. Sales of IPAs have skyrocketed worldwide. Some breweries have even started slapping the abbreviation "IPA" onto any old hoppy beer in the hope of boosting sales. As brewers explore more bitter tastes in beer, it seems likely that the IPA will remain a popular choice. Beer drinkers sometimes equate hoppiness with quality, which is one reason why IPAs continue to get stronger.

Punk IPA

Style: *INDIA PALE ALE*

ABV: *5.6%*　　**Producer:** *Brewdog*
Fermentation: *Top*　　**Locality:** *Ellon*
Bottle: *11 fl oz (0.33 l) with a crown cap*　　*(Scotland – UK)*

This iconic beer, made by James Watt and Martin Dickie, the brewing bad boys behind Scotland's Brewdog Brewery, is a contemporary reinterpretation of an IPA.

Once upon a time, beers like this—made mainly with American hops—were always labeled American IPAs. Today, however, thanks in part to Punk IPA, this outdated classification no longer applies to all IPAs brewed using American hops. On the label, Brewdog calls this one a "Post Modern Classic," emphasizing its British roots while also acknowledging its use of new-world hops and flavors.

Brewdog is almost better known for its marketing antics than it is for its beers. James Watt and Martin Dickie once projected naked images of themselves onto the Houses of Parliament. You read that correctly. But marketing controversies aside, their Punk IPA has been an inspiration to IPA-brewers the world over.

Profile

Appearance: *deep, golden color; slightly hazy,
with a moderately persistent white head*
Aroma: *malt, caramel, resin, exotic fruit (mango and pineapple),
lemon peel, with spicy notes*
Mouthfeel: *bitter hops, orange pith, notes of pink grapefruit, plus all the flavors
promised by the aroma*
Overall Impression: *very bitter character, but never too strong;
extremely drinkable*

TORPEDO
65 IBU

SIERRA NEVADA

TORPEDO

EXTRA IPA

alc. 7.2% vol.

SIERRA NEVADA BREWING CO. CHICO, CA & MILLS RIVER, NC USA

Torpedo

Style: *INDIA PALE ALE*

ABV: *7.2%*　　**Producer:** *Sierra Nevada Brewing Co.*
Fermentation: *Top*　　**Locality:** *Chico*
Bottle: *12 fl oz (0.355 l) with a crown cap*　　*(California – USA)*

Sierra Nevada Brewing Co. is a legendary California enterprise and one of the first American "beer renaissance" breweries. Founded in the early 1980s, it has expanded in step with the American craft beer movement. Considered the birthplace of the APA (American Pale Ale), it has transformed the global beer industry with its use of American hops.

Torpedo was born out of the idea to use dry hopping to enhance hop aromas and hop bitterness. It rejuvenated Sierra Nevada's image as an innovator, as many beer enthusiasts had begun thinking that the brewery had been limiting itself to traditional beers for far too long.

In truth, Torpedo isn't nearly as bitter as many other IPAs currently on the market, but its flavors are bold and beautiful. It uses whole-cone American hops that blend well with the tastes of pine and citrus.

Profile
Appearance: *slightly hazy amber color, with a moderately persistent, beige white head*
Aroma: *malt, caramel, resin, citrus fruits (mainly grapefruit and lemon), with grassy notes and a floral sensation that fades quickly*
Mouthfeel: *more resinous and caramelly than citrusy, but it delivers on the promises made by its aroma; a long, dry finish dominated by hops; ends with a malty sweetness*
Overall Impression: *great balance between malty sweetness and the resinous/herbaceous flavor of hops; bitter, but never overpowering; very drinkable despite its high alcohol content*

LIQUID *DIPA*
FEAR

LA PIRATA BREWING

Liquid Fear

Style: *INDIA PALE ALE (DOUBLE IPA)*

ABV: *8.7%*
Fermentation: *Top*
Can: *14.8 fl oz (0.44 l)*

Producer: *La Pirata Brewing*
Locality: *Súria*
(Barcelona – Spain)

La Pirata Brewing, a Spanish brewery, is a great example of how beer—in this case beer strongly influenced by US craft breweries—has become popular even in countries without significant beer-brewing traditions.

Liquid Fear is proof that a Double IPA can be successfully brewed on Spanish soil. The name "Liquid Fear" is an homage to the sociologist Zygmunt Bauman, who wrote a book with the same title. This Double IPA may be an attempt to explode our notions of what an IPA can do, perhaps also challenging the cultural homogenization and consumerism Bauman wrote about in his books. Another postmodern take on the IPA in the same vein as Brewdog's Punk IPA. Overall, a great choice for anyone seeking a sweeter, more lively interpretation of an IPA.

Profile

Appearance: *bright amber, hazy, with a receding beige head*

Aroma: *caramel, exotic fruit (mango and maracuja), lemon peel, mandarin, with spicy and resinous notes*

Mouthfeel: *velvety, with some of the flavors promised by the aroma; predominantly mango, maracuja, and caramel, with a long, resinous, and bitter finish*

Overall Impression: *fairly balanced; pleasant and easy-to-drink despite its high alcohol content*

Grätze: Sottsass, Piano,
Boccioni, Manzoni,
Grignani,
Fontana, Rossi,
Scarpa &
Vignelli.
Grät

Other Cereal Grains

By law in most countries, beer must contain a minimum percentage of malt, though this percentage can vary from country to country. There are also many traditional beer recipes that require cereal grains other than barley. Belgium has Wit/Blanche beers and Lambics, for example. Germany boasts Weissbier (or Weizenbier) wheat beers and their many variants (Dunkel Weissbier, Weizenbock, etc.), Roggenbiers (which use rye instead of wheat), Gose beers, and Berliner Weisses. Breweries in the United States brew just about every wheat beer in existence. In Poland, they brew a beer style called Piwo Grodziskie, which is made with smoked wheat. Below you'll find three very different wheat styles to give you an idea of just how diverse this group is.

• *Witbiers* (or *Blanche* beers, in French) are sharp-tasting Belgian beers characterized by the use of 50% unmalted wheat, orange peel, coriander, and yeast strains that create haziness and the right esters (chemical compounds derived from acids).

• *Weizenbocks* (German beers) are the strongest and richest version of the classic Weissbier. They contain a high quantity of wheat, although the wheat is malted. These tend to be malty, high-alcohol beers with fruity esters (usually banana).

• *Piwo Grodziskie* are traditional Polish beers typically brewed in the city of Grodzisk (Grätz in German; in Germany this style is known as *Grätzer*). Grodziskie beers usually have lower alcohol contents. They're characterized by the use of 100% smoked wheat, which gives them a delicate, smoky flavor.

Fleur Sofronia

Style: *BLANCHE + HIBISCUS*

ABV: *5%*　　**Producer:** *MC77*
Fermentation: *Top*　　**Locality:** *Serrapetrona, Macerata*
Bottle: *11 fl oz (0.33 l) with a crown cap*　　*(Le Marche – Italy)*

MC77 is a brewery in Le Marche, Italy. It was founded in 2013 by beer and homebrewing enthusiasts Cecilia Scisciani and Matteo Pomposini, who decided to turn their passion for homebrewing into a full-time job. They've made a big spalsh in the Italian beer scene and have won several prizes, including a gold medal from the European Beer Star Awards.

Fleur Sofronia is MC77's take on the classic Blanche style. The spiciness tyical of Blanches is elegantly enriched here by the addition of whole hibiscus flowers from North Africa. MC77's brave use of exotic ingredients has made them a must-watch brewery and helped them clinch 2019's Beer of the Year Award presented by the Italian beer organization Fermento Birra.

Profile

Appearance: *deep pink, hazy; an abundant white head*
with pinkish highlights that fades quickly
Aroma: *a delicate, herbaceous aroma packed with spices; notes of mandarin,*
hibiscus, and fresh flowers
Mouthfeel: *an inviting sourness is followed by the same floral sensations found*
in the aroma; enriched by a light saltiness that goes well with the fruity notes;
the finish is slightly acidic and leaves a nice, clean feeling in the mouth
Overall Impression: *stunningly elegant in color, aroma, and taste;*
its light body and unobtrusive carbonation complete the experienc;
a unique reinterpretation of the classic Blanche style

Aventinus Tap 6

Style: *WEIZEN(DOPPEL)BOCK*

ABV: *8.2%*
Fermentation: *Top*
Bottle: *11 fl oz (0.33 l) with a crown cap*

Producer: *G. Schneider & Sohn*
Locality: *Kelheim*
(Lower Bavaria – Germany)

G. Schneider & Sohn is a legendary German brewery in Bavaria. It was founded in 1872 by Georg Schneider I and is still in the hands of the Schneider family (its current owner is Georg Schneider VI). The brewery specializes in wheat beers produced with locally grown wheat. Its enduring popularity helped it survive both World Wars, and to this day it still makes use of traditional German brewing methods.

Aventinus Tap 6 is a unique version of a Weizenbock. Born in 1907, it was the first Weizenbock in Bavaria and is still the oldest-known wheat Doppelbock (Weizendoppelbock). It's been described as "a caramel poem" and "the best beer to drink while sitting in front of a fireplace." If you've never tried a Weizenbock before, this is the one to start with.

Profile

Appearance: *slightly hazy brown color with ruby-red highlights; a moderately persistent light-beige head*

Aroma: *bread crust, raisins, ripe plum, banana, and caramel*

Mouthfeel: *the flavors promised by the aroma are all there—banana, caramel, bread crust, raisins and plum, plus the addition of pear; great overall balance, with a warm finish accompanied by hints of clove*

Overall Impression: *a complex, satisfying beer with a barely perceptible bitterness that leaves a feeling of fullness and satisfaction in the mouth; a true classic that all beer lovers should try at least once*

Grätze: Sottsass, Piano,
Boccioni, Manzoni,
Grignani,
Fontana, Rossi,
Scarpa &
Vignelli.
Grätze mille.

Grätze Mille
Grätze-style Ale Brewed
with Oranges, 11.2 fl oz.

A salty, sour and smoky experience. Brewed to
honour the boot country, with zesty orange,
oranges per 1000 liters. Grazie mille...

Grätze Mille

Style: *GRODZISKIE*

ABV: *4%*   **Producer:** *To Øl*
Fermentation: *Top*   **Locality:** *Copenhagen*
Bottle: *11 fl oz (0.33 l) with a crown cap*   *(Denmark)*

To Øl is a Danish microbrewery project from Tore Gynther. Tore started out as a homebrewer in 2005, brewing beers in his high school's kitchen while still a student. In 2010, he founded To Øl. For a few years, To Øl was solely a "gipsy brewer," meaning it didn't own its own facility or equipment and thus had to rent space from other breweries. After years of experimentation, To Øl finally opened its own brewing facility in 2019: To Øl City, which is located in Svinninge, Denmark.

Grätze Mille is a Grodziskie with added rye and lots of oranges. Using so many oranges gives this one a uniqely Italian flare, hence the name, which is a play on words between the style and the Italian expression *grazie mille* ("thank you very much").

The label is a personal tribute to numerous well-known Italian designers, artists, and architects. It was designed by Kasper Ledet, who oversees all visual aspects of To Øl's operation.

Profile

Appearance: *straw-yellow color, cloudy, with a thin, white head that fades quickly*
Aroma: *the citrus fruits (mainly oranges) blend nicely with a purée of yellow fruits; includes hints of biscuit and smoked scamorza cheese*
Mouthfeel: *the unobtrusive smoky sensation persists, balanced by light acidity; this eventually gives way to biscuit, citrus fruits, and a herbaceous finish*
Overall Impression: *an interesting reinterpretation of a Grodziskie; smoked wheat shouldn't go well with the freshness of oranges, but it absolutely does here; the rye malt adds a sour note*

Borderline Beers

This section is full of oddball beers that don't fit neatly into any established category. Most were created to blow the minds of enthusiasts, with little regard for marketability or long-term potential. In creating products like these, brewers give themselves the opportunity to break free from beer doctrine and track down the flavors our palates didn't even know they were craving. Designing and producing cutting-edge beers isn't all fun and games, though. At the end of the day, breweries are real businesses, so it's not uncommon for even the bravest among them to balance their Frankenstein creations with batches of the brews they know people will buy, as this helps them keep the doors open. The beers featured here are characterized by strange ingredients, inventive processes, and risky combinations. Perhaps the only thing they all have in common is the desire to provoke. In almost every case, the brewers behind the beer based it on a recognizable style. Should classic styles remain as they are, frozen in time, or do they have room for improvement? Every brewing operation today must wrestle with this question each time they're deciding on their next batch.

Taste buds change. Trends come and go. New, more efficient brewing techniques slowly crowd out established ones. This section is a nod to the creative spirit of brewers everywhere. Without their bravery and inventiveness, we would still be stuck drinking the same mass-produced beers our parents drank. Here's to the end of that dismal era.

Chocolate Chiplote Cloud

ABV: *12.5%*
Fermentation: *Top*
Bottle: *11 fl oz (0.33 l) with a crown cap*

Producer: *Brewski*
Locality: *Helsingborg (Sweden)*

Founded in Sweden in 2014, Brewski makes exploring the limits of beer something to be proud of. The use of fresh fruit in their recipes is a leitmotif in their creations. They are convinced that just because a beer has never been made before doesn't mean it can't be done, and their brews often push boundaries.

Chocolate Chipotle Cloud is an Imperial Stout with an extremely cheeky label. In theory, a toilet with a mushroom cloud shooting out of it shouldn't make a beer appetizing, but Brewski somehow manages to pull it off. Here the challenge was to discover whether consumers were ready for a little heat in their beers. Challenge accepted.

Profile

Appearance: *dark brown color, slightly hazy, with a fairly persistent, beige head*

Aroma: *roasted malt, cocoa powder, hints of vegetables, slightly metallic*

Mouthfeel: *the persistent hotness is balanced by the sweetness; the cocoa powder mimics the sensation of eating a chili chocolate bar; the finish is dry, and the high alcohol content is warming without being overwhelming*

Overall Impression: *as Brewski asks on the label (translated): "Do you have the stamina to stay and tough it out? Or will you leave this stout for those of a stronger build?" We accepted the challenge and are very satisfied with the brew*

Ristretto Negroni

ABV: *6.7%*
Fermentation: *Top*
Bottle: *11 fl oz (0.33 l) with a crown cap*

Producer: *Siren Craft Brew*
Locality: *Wokingham (UK)*

Siren Craft Brew was founded in 2013 with the intention of exploring all kinds of wild ingredients. Ristretto Negroni is part of Project Barista (started in 2017), which aims to brew beer with coffee procured solely from independent roasters.

Ristretto Negroni combines two passions of the brewery's founder: coffee and the Negroni cocktail. It is a Brut IPA brewed with licorice root, with the addition of hibiscus flowers (for coloring), orange juice and peel, juniper, and cilantro. A real homage to the Negroni, as well as to Rwanda Vunga coffee. This is definitely an interesting borderline beer, though we can't resist asking: why would a coffee lover want orange peels in their drink? And why would a Negroni lover want to mix in coffee? Siren's answer: who cares, we did it anyway, drink up.

Profile

Appearance: *golden yellow leaning towards orange, with a coppery head that fades quickly*
Aroma: *coffee, licorice, black tea leaves, orange peel, and juniper*
Mouthfeel: *slightly sour; the coffee and licorice overwhelm the juniper and cilantro, though they gradually become apparent; bitter aftertaste and dry finish*
Overall Impression: *a provocation, indeed; this one is such a complex IPA that it risks leaving you a little perplexed*

Mûre-Rullquin

ABV: *6%*
Fermentation: *Mixed*
Bottle: *25 fl oz (0.75 l) with a cork stopper*

Producer: *Brasserie Artisanale de Rulles/ Gueuzerie Tilquin*
Locality: *Habay/Rebeck (Belgium)*

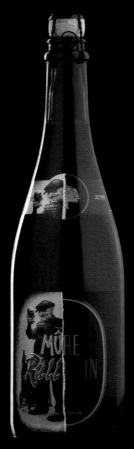

Rulles and Tilquin are two pillars of the Belgian new wave. They're helping traditional styles take a step forward and start the new millennium with freshness and innovation.

Brasserie de Rulles is the creation of Grégory Verhelst, a brewer who—at the beginning of the 2000s—began producing classic styles with avant-garde hopping techniques. Pierre Tilquin is Wallonia-based master blender of Lambics. He buys wort from producers in Pajottenland and Brussels and ferments and ages it in the barrels of his Gueuzerie Tilquin blendery. His approach to a sacred product like Lambic is based on respect for tradition, though he manages to sneak in a touch of experimentation. Mûre-Rullquin is a blend of 7/8 Rulles Brune and 1/8 young Lambic from Tilquin (8 months in the barrel). Before being matured for a further 6 months in the bottle, Mûre-Rullquin is refermented with blackberries (9 oz/2.1 pints/260 g/l).

Profile
Appearance: *dark-brown color with purplish highlights; fading head; an abundance of yeast sediment at the bottom*

Aroma: *wild notes (wood, dust, cellar), fruit, caramel, light-roasted malt, vinous*

Mouthfeel: *thin, acidic body; red fruit, caramel, roasted malt, wood*

Overall Impression: *Brune di Rulles succeeds in softening the exuberance and roughness of Tilquin's young Lambic; the blackberries, with their sweet acidity, add an additional sensorial level to this beer*

Miss Liken

ABV: *8%*
Fermentation: *Top*
Bottle: *25 fl oz (0.75 l) with a crown cap*

Producer: *Birrificio BioNoć - Birre Della Terra*
Locality: *Mezzano (Trentino – Italy)*

BioNoć derives its name from the nicknames of its founders: Fabio Simoni (Bio) and Nicola Simion (Noc). The brewery has been located in the mountainous Primiero valley (in Italy) since 2013. It has a close relationship with the area. The brewery has four lines of beers: permanent beers (traditional styles), seasonal beers (special styles produced occasionally), sour beers (aged in wood barrels under the supervision of Nicola Coppe), and "beers of the land."

The beers in the latter category are made with cereal grains and hops grown by Stonebreaker Farm in the Berici hills. In addition to cereal grains (barley, rye, and wheat) and Trentino hops, Miss Liken also contains an unusual (but still local) ingredient: lichen, which is a slow-growing plant that forms on rocks and trees. Lichen represents the symboiotic relationship between this brewery and its environment.

Miss Liken was created by chef patron Alessandro Gilmozzi of the Michelin-star restaurant El Molin in Cavalese, a fantastic representative of Italian mountain cuisine. El Molin has been using lichen in its dishes for years.

Profile

Appearance: *straw color, hazy; persistent white head*
Aroma: *ripe fruit, complex spiciness, notes of undergrowth*
Mouthfeel: *round body, red fruit; slightly citrusy and balsamic*
Overall Impression: *while oozing classic Belgium from every pore, it guides your taste buds into the unknown*

Mexicake

ABV: *11%*
Fermentation: *Top*
Bottle: *11 fl oz (0.33 l) with a crown cap*

Producer: *Tempest Brewing Company*
Locality: *Galashiels (UK)*

Tempest Brewing Co. was born in 2010 as the passion project of two friends who moved to Scotland from New Zealand. In Scotland, they bought a small abandoned farm to start brewing beer. They expanded in 2014, and in 2018 they were recognized by RateBeer.com as one of the best breweries in the world.

The idea behind Mexicake was to reconstruct a cake inside a beer. This one's an Imperial Stout brewed with vanilla pods, Sri Lankan cinnamon, top-quality cocoa, and mulato and chipotle peppers. A spicy, aromatic Mexican cake in a bottle. The innovation here lies in packing in so many ingredients while still maintaining control of the profile. Tempest pulls it off beautifully.

Profile

Appearance: *pitch black, with a quickly fading head the color of a friar's habit*

Aroma: *vanilla, cocoa, roasted coffee; the aroma of the chili peppers emerges gradually, along with a hint of cinnamon*

Mouthfeel: *chocolate, coffee, and a little heat from the chilies; as the beer warms up, the cinnamon, vanilla, and heat get stronger and more persistent; the alcohol enhances the heat without overpowering the brew*

Overall Impression: *an interesting, balanced, and well-made Imperial Stout; the ingredients blend well in the mixture, while the hotness isn't overbearing; everything is in its place—a real pleasure to drink*

Kameradski Balsamico

ABV: *12.5%*
Fermentation: *Mixed*
Bottle: *11 fl oz (0.33 l) with a crown cap*

Producer: *Brouwerij 't Verzet*
Locality: *Anzegem (Belgium)*

Alex Lippens and Koen Van Lancker met in college and bonded over a shared love of homebrewing. Young and penniless, but still determined, they worked in various breweries to gain experience. In 2011, they founded their own beer firm and were immediately noticed by beer critics and the public. In 2016, after 5 years of hard work, they managed to turn their firm into an independent brewery, which they opened in their hometown. The name "'t Verzet" roughly translates to "the Resistance," possibly intended as a reminder that never giving up makes it possible to reach your goals. Or perhaps the name represents their desire to resist stagnation in the beer industry and create original, revolutionary brews with character, just like this Balsamic Kameradski. This one is a blend that combines two distinct styles and two distinct production philosophies (an Imperial Stout and a 3-year, oak-aged Oud Bruin). The result is a wonderfully balanced product that transcends its ingredients. Sweetness and sourness are mortal enemies, but in this beer they sit comfortably beside each other on a velvet sofa.

Profile
Appearance: *very dark brown; a fine thin head with a dense, light-brown color*
Aroma: *cocoa, blackberries, blueberries, raspberries, balsamic vinegar*
Mouthfeel: *dense and smooth; fruit chocolate; sweet followed by sour, with an acidic finish*
Overall Impression: *sweet and sour intermingle inside a chocolatey dungeon*

Italian Tomato Ale

ABV: *4.5%*
Fermentation: *Top*
Bottle: *11 fl oz (0.33 l) with a crown cap*

Producer: *Carrobiolo*
Locality: *Monza*
(Lombardy – Italy)

The Carrobiolo Brewery likes contradictions. Brewer Matteo Bonfanti enjoys tinkering with classic beer recipes to produce "toy" beers. This beer was born around the same time as Carrobiolo's Porcini Imperial Stout. It's intended as a response to the many aromatic beers that use artificial ingredients instead of real ones. It makes use of the classic Italian ingredients for pizza: cereal grains, tomatoes, oregano, and basil. The inclusion of tomato may scare a few folks away, but fear not. When you smell the aroma of this one, you'll be amazed. The taste is even better. The Datterini tomatoes, harvested during the summer at their peak ripeness, are processed raw just like they are for tomato sauce. They are then immediately fermented with the wort and brewed without their skins (like Pinot Nero grapes in Champagne) to obtain a lighter-colored beer. Oregano and basil, well dosed in different proportions, are added during brewing and then added again—fresh—at the end of the fermentation process. A gourmet beer that will blow your mind.

Profile

Appearance: *golden-yellow color, clear, with a white head that fades quickly*
Aroma: *pizza margherita (tomato, oregano, baked white bread)*
Mouthfeel: *thin body, slight acidity; ripe tomato, with a minty sensation*
Overall Impression: *if beer is liquid bread, then this beer is liquid pizza*

Péché Mortel

ABV: *9.5%*   **Producer:** *Brasserie Dieu du Ciel!*

Fermentation: *Top*   **Locality:** *Montreal*

Bottle: *11.5 fl oz (0.341 l)*   *(Québec – Canada)*

Dieu du Ciel! (This phrase is used to express amazement, so it demands an exclamation mark.) was born in 1998 as a small brewpub. It was founded by microbiologist and homebrewer Jean Francois Gravel. Over the years, it has become a Canadian beer landmark. It expanded in 2007, moving its production to a new location (an abandoned supermarket) separate from the brewpub. Since the expansion, Dieu du Ciel! has transformed into an absolute worldwide benchmark for brewing quality, perseverance, and creativity.

If Coffee Imperial Stout is now considered a style in its own right, then Péché Mortel (first made in 2001) should also be considered its own unique style, or at least a brewing milestone. It's full yet fluid, intense yet simple, alcoholic yet gentle, and it tastes as if both hot and cold infusions of coffee were used in the brew. It's almost a mortal sin not to enjoy this one.

Profile

Appearance: *a dark-brown, almost black color; a fine and persistent cappuccino-colored head*

Aroma: *roasted coffee, coffee drupe, dark malts, licorice root, tobacco*

Mouthfeel: *medium body, excellent carbonation; espresso coffee, French-press coffee, coffee liqueur, cocoa, and molasses; sweet and bitter; light astringency and acidity*

Overall Impression: *those who prefer coffee to beer should give this one a try so they can see what they're missing*

17.03 Insa
Pete's Dark Past

ABV: *7%* **Producer:** *Northern Monk*
Fermentation: *Top* **Locality:** *Leeds*
Can: *14.8 fl oz (0.44 l)*   *(UK)*

Northern Monk Brewery was founded in 2014 in Leeds, England. Its mission is to produce innovative beers inspired by the history of monastic brewing, which has been practiced across the region for thousands of years. Their desire to give space to artists, athletes, and local personalities led to the Patrons Project. Seven limited-edition canned beers are produced for each series in the project, and every edition gets a new label.

Pete's Dark Past is part of series 17. It celebrates Insa, a globally recognized street artist from Leeds who incorporates new technologies into his works. ks. Beer number 3 is a Chocolate, Caramel & Biscuit Stout. While the name of this one makes it sound sinister, the brew itself is very balanced and pleasant. Just like some of Insa's artistic pieces, this one requires an open mind to be fully appreciated.

Profile
Appearance: *impenetrable dark-brown color; a light-brown head that fades quickly*
Aroma: *vanilla predominates, then caramel, chocolate, barley coffee, and roasted hazelnuts*
Mouthfeel: *full, velvety body; all the flavors promised by the aroma are there; a pleasantly dry finish with a little bitterness; nicely balanced by just the right amount of sweetness*
Overall Impression: *a complex-yet-pleasant beer available only to the lucky few who manage to snag a can*

Original Raspberry Meringue Ice Cream Pie

ABV: *6%*

Fermentation: *Top*

Can: *14.8 fl oz (0.44 l)*

Producer: *Omnipollo®*

+ Buxton Brewery

Locality: *Stockholm (Sweden) + Buxton (UK)*

The Omnipollo® beer production company was born in Sweden in 2010. It was founded by brewer Henok Fentie and artist Karl Grandin. The combination of beer and pop culture gives life to this gipsy brewery, which makes its beers in collaboration with other breweries around the world. Their provocative recipes and marketing techniques are an inspiration to many up-and-coming brewers.

Original Raspberry Meringue Ice Cream Pie, with its fanciful label, is a shockingly drinkable experiment. Beers like this one make you stop and think about where exactly the border is between beer and dessert. Raspberry juice, vanilla, and lactose are expertly blended here by Omnipollo®'s longtime friends at Buxton Brewery in England (experts in the use of unconventional ingredients). This one's inspired by cake and ice cream, yet it's categorized as a Fruit Beer. Go figure!

Profile

Appearance: *deep pink, slightly hazy, with a fairly persistent, dusty, pink-colored head*

Aroma: *raspberry, vanilla; notes of citric acid*

Mouthfeel: *the moderate citric acidity gives way to the fullness of the lactose; the raspberries are evident, as is the vanilla; the finish is long and smooth*

Overall Impression: *blurs the line between dessert and beer; fanciful and captivating; a great example of the gypsy brewery trend*

Pillars of Light Peach Milkshake IPA

ABV: *7.5%*
Fermentation: *Top*
Can: *14.8 fl oz (0.44 l)*

Producer: *Amundsen Brewery*
Locality: *Oslo*
(Norway)

Amundsen is currently the largest craft brewery in Norway. It started out as a brewpub in 2011, with a very modest 132-gallon (5 hl) brewing facility, but it's since grown exponentially. This is thanks to the quality of its craft brewing and the stellar designs on the labels it releases.

Their Milkshake IPAs, including Pillars of Light Peach, are great examples of their approach: well-made, innovative beers supported by sharp label designs. Although perhaps slightly less interesting than other beers under the Milkshake IPA umbrella, Pillars of Light Peach is a master class in how to deploy fresh fruit, vanilla, and lactose in an IPA.

Profile

Appearance: *golden-yellow color, cloudy, with a thin white head that fades quickly*

Aroma: *peach, vanilla, tropical fruit (papaya, passion fruit); herbaceous notes*

Mouthfeel: *the round smoothness of the lactose enhances the notes of vanilla and peach; the aroma of the hops and their herbaceous components overpower the persistent finish*

Overall Impression: *pleasant to drink, full, fresh, herbaceous; an easygoing beer; its strength lies in its freshness and in its masterfully balanced flavors*

Even More Candy Bars ed. 4

ABV: *14.4%*
Fermentation: *Top*
Can: *16 fl oz (0.473 l)*

Producer: *Evil Twin Brewing*
Locality: *Copenhagen (Denmark) /
Ridgewood (New York – USA)*

EVEN MORE CANDY BARS
EDITION 4

Evil Twin Brewing was born as a gipsy brewery in Denmark in 2010 (meaning it initially had no facilities of its own). In 2019, it finally opened a facility in NYC. Evil Twin is well-known for putting creative spins on traditional recipes.

The fourth installment in its Even More Candy Bars series is a prime example. This highly alcoholic Imperial Stout (or rather, Pastry Stout) is dry-hopped with a whopping 200 lb (about 90 kg) of Kit Kats. While not their most extreme beer, the idea to use a recognizable commercial product in an original brew is laudably daring. No desperate struggle to source local ingredients here, as Kit Kats can go straight from the supermarket shelf into the fermenter.

Profile

Appearance: *pitch-black color, with a fairly persistent, light-brown head*

Aroma: *milk chocolate, caramel, vanilla, and hints of burnt coffee*

Mouthfeel: *surprisingly rich choclate flavor for Kit Kats; enriched with notes of coffee and caramel; slightly resinous sensation from the hops; the alcohol is warming, but the brew is still uncommonly smooth*

Overall Impression: *full body, unobtrusive alcohol, chocolate that mingles with the coffee; a really enjoyable Imperial Stout from start to finish*

Lemon Sherbet

ABV: *6%*
Fermentation: *Mixed*
Can: *11 fl oz (0.33 l)*

Producer: *Coolhead - Pühaste - Zagovor (collaboration)*
Locality: *Tuusula (Finland)*

CoolHead was founded in 2016 in Tuusula, which is about 19 miles (30 km) from Helsinki. Its mission is to produce Sours, IPAs, and beers with high alcohol contents, including many barrel-aged brews. CoolHead describes its philosophy as a clash between Nordic minimalism and the colorful, stimulating flavors of the tropics. This is best reflected through odd pairings such as licorice and bananas, or coconut and sage.

Lemon Sherbet, created together with the breweries Pühaste (Estonia) and Zagovor (Russia), is a Double Dry Hopped Imperial Berliner Weisse, meaning it's a "super" Berliner Weisse with double the alcohol content, twice the dry-hopping (with citrus fruits), and the addition of fresh lemon zest and coriander seeds. Lactose and oats, with their softness and silky smooth characteristics, are used to help achieve a consistency similar to that of sherbet.

Profile

Appearance: *bright-yellow color, opalescent; white head with large bubbles*
Aroma: *lemon, lemon zest, lemon rind, lemon juice*
Mouthfeel: *intense citric acidity; the grassy bitterness of dandelion; citrusy and spicy, with very high carbonation*
Overall Impression: *an innovative beer with the character of a digestif*

Cherry Bubble Gum

ABV: *4.5%*

Fermentation: *Top*

Can: *11 fl oz (0.33 l)*

Producer: *Duckpond Brewing*

Locality: *Gothenburg (Sweden)*

In 2013, Nikola Šarčević, leader of the Swedish punk band Millencolin, founded a small brewery called Mikrofonbryggeriet in Gothenburg, Sweden. In 2019, it changed its name to Duckpond Brewing, but it still continues to create beers with experimental recipes inspired by cocktails, desserts, and ingredients that usually have little to do with beer.

Cherry Bubble Gum—a Berliner Weisse made to taste like, you guessed it, cherries and bubble gum—is a good example of the odd beers in its experimental line. The ingredients aren't listed on the label (only the allergens), so we don't know where the bubble gum flavor comes from. Although a beautiful beverage to look at and very pleasant to drink, it remains a little too square in its unconventionality. However, its underlying concept is brilliant, and ultimately it's an interesting reinterpretation of the classic aromas traditionally used in Berliner Weisse beers.

Profile

Appearance: *beetroot color, cloudy, with an abundant, pink head that fades quickly*

Aroma: *predominantly bubble gum, followed by caramel and cherry yogurt*

Mouthfeel: *cherry and bubble gum slightly overwhelm everything else; the citric acid and thin body lighten the sensation of cherry syrup; the acidulous finish leaves a pleasant sensation in the mouth*

Overall Impression: *a fresh and balanced brew despite the heaviness of the artificial flavor of bubble gum; an experiment that pushes the boundaries of beer without feeling gimmicky*

Biographies

Pietro Fontana is the owner of renowned microbrewery Piccolo Opificio Brassicolo del Carrobiolo Fermentum in Monza, Italy. In addition to producing award-winning craft beers with local ingredients, he organizes brewing courses and events and spends as much time as possible promoting beer culture. He is the author of *Beer Sommelier: A Journey Through the Culture of Beer*, also published by White Star.

Fabio Petroni is a photographer specializing in portraits and still lifes. He works with numerous international businesses and advertising agencies, always bringing his own unique approach to each shoot and ad campaign. He is a frequent collaborator with White Star and has provided photographs for many of their illustrated books.

Acknowledgements

The author wishes to thank Efrem Borroni for the indispensable help he provided while this book was being written.

He would also like to thank Brasserie Indipendante and Pane Liquido for providing him with beer bottles and cans.

Photo Credits

All photographs are by Fabio Petroni unless noted below:

Cover: gioiak2/123RF; page 2: Shutterstock.com; page 7: DeAgostini/Getty Images; page 8: Hulton Archive/Getty Images; pages 21-22 and 23: Shutterstock.com.

Project Editor • VALERIA MANFERTO DE FABIANIS

Graphic Design • MARIA CUCCHI

WHITE STAR PUBLISHERS

White Star Publishers® is a trademark owned by White Star s.r.l.

© 2020 White Star s.r.l.
Piazzale Luigi Cadorna, 6
20123 Milan, Italy
www.whitestar.it

ISBN 978-88-544-1691-8
1 2 3 4 5 6   24 23 22 21 20

Translation: TperTradurre s.r.l.

Printed in Croatia